Practice Papers for SQA Exams

Higher

Modern Studies

© 2016 Leckie & Leckie Ltd
Cover image © ink-tank

001/23022016

10 9 8 7 6 5 4 3 2 1

ISBN 9780007590971

Published by
Leckie & Leckie Ltd
An imprint of HarperCollins*Publishers*
Westerhill Road, Bishopbriggs, Glasgow, G64 2QT
T: 0844 576 8126   F: 0844 576 8131
leckieandleckie@harpercollins.co.uk
www.leckieandleckie.co.uk

Commissioning Editor: Katherine Wilkinson
Project Manager: Craig Balfour

Special thanks to
Louise Robb (copyedit and proofread)
QBS (layout and diagrams)

Printed in Italy by Grafica Veneta S.P.A.

A CIP Catalogue record for this book is available from
the British Library.

Acknowledgements

We would like to thank the following for permission to
reproduce their material:

Extract on page 10 reproduced courtesy of *The
Huffington Post*

Extract on page 12 reproduced courtesy of *YouGov*

Extract on page 14 reproduced courtesy of Emily
Thornberry MP for *The Huffington Post*

Extract on page 15 reproduced courtesy of *The
Guardian, copyright Guardian News & Media Ltd 2016*

Extract on pages 21-22 reproduced courtesy of *The
Telegraph, copyright Telegraph Media Group Ltd, 2016*

Extract on page 27 reproduced courtesy of *The
Telegraph, copyright Telegraph Media Group Ltd, 2016*

Extract on page 33 reproduced courtesy of *The New
Statesman*

Whilst every effort has been made to trace the copyright
holders, in cases where this has been unsuccessful, or if
any have inadvertently been overlooked, the Publishers
would gladly receive any information enabling them to
rectify any error or omission at the first opportunity.

Introduction

This book is to help you with your preparations for the Higher Modern Studies exam. It contains three practice papers which show the layout of the exam, the question types and an idea of how each of the different types of questions are marked. You may wish to dip into the papers as you study a certain topic but it's probably a good idea to sit a whole paper nearer the exam so you get an idea of the time pressure involved.

Course and question paper structure

Higher Modern Studies is marked out of 90. The question paper is worth 60 marks and the Assignment is worth 30 marks. In the question paper there are three sections, each worth 20 marks:

- Democracy in Scotland and the United Kingdom – refer to either or both.

- Social Issues in the United Kingdom – complete questions on **EITHER** Social Inequality **OR** Crime and the Law.

- International Issues – complete questions on a World Power **OR** a World Issue.

Make sure you know which option you have studied

For the third section, you will have studied a G20 country for World Powers such as the USA or China. The questions asked will not refer specifically to the USA or China but will say 'For a world power you have studied'. Alternatively, if you have studied a World Issue such as Terrorism, the question will not specifically mention that but will say 'For a world issue you have studied'.

The first thing you should write down is what World Power or World Issue you have studied **before** you start to answer the question.

Paper structure

In total you will complete 5 questions in 2 hours 15 minutes:

- 2 × 12-mark knowledge questions.

- 1 × 20-mark knowledge question.

- 2 × 8-mark skills questions.

Question types

Knowledge questions

Knowledge questions are either for 12 marks or for 20 marks.

12-mark questions

For 12-mark questions, 8 marks are given for knowledge and 4 marks for analysis/evaluation. If more than 4 analysis/evaluation marks are available, these can be credited as knowledge and understanding (KU) if required.

Analyse questions – Candidates will identify parts of an issue, the relationship between these parts and their relationships with the whole; draw out and relate implications.

Evaluate questions – Candidates will make a judgement based on criteria; determine the value of something.

20-mark questions

For 20-mark questions, 8 marks are given for knowledge, 4 for analysis/evaluation, 6 for conclusions and 2 for structure

Discuss questions – Candidates will communicate ideas and information on the issue in the statement. Candidates will be credited for analysing and evaluating different views of the statement/viewpoint.

You must show knowledge, analysis, evaluation and show a clear, coherent structure – think introduction, paragraphs and a final conclusion but also that your points are made in a logical and coherent order.

To what extent questions – Candidates will analyse the issue in the question and come to a conclusion or conclusions that involve an evaluative judgement that is likely to be quantitative in nature.

You must show knowledge, analysis, evaluation and show a clear, coherent structure – think introduction, paragraphs and a final conclusion but also that your points are made in a logical and coherent order.

Skills questions

These will appear in the section where there is not a 20-mark essay. They are worth 8 marks.

Drawing conclusions questions

You will be asked to draw **two** conclusions on a subject. Depending on the amount of evidence you use from the three sources, you can gain up to 3 marks per conclusion. Try and link evidence from different sources or indeed within different parts of the same source. In order to gain full marks you will need to come to an overall conclusion on the issue **AND** use all the sources. No marks are awarded for just the conclusions without any evidence.

To what extent is the view accurate questions

You are asked to identify, using all three sources, where the given view is correct or not. Again, for the full 8 marks, you must make an overall judgement as to whether the view is supported by evidence.

You can also gain 2 additional marks for any comment or evaluation of the sources used. If any source is adapted, it must be stated that it is unreliable as you don't know how it has been adapted. Try to use words like reliable, out-of-date, bias, useful.

Handy hints

Be organised

Boring as it may be, organisation is the key to success. Make sure your folder is organised – put all your notes and information into the right unit section. Make sure that you look at essays and skills questions that you have done and understand the feedback your teacher has given you. If you don't, go back and ask them.

Remember it's **Modern** Studies – your World Issues, all evidence and examples quoted should come from the last 10 years at the very latest.

You will have one 20-mark essay question to do, 2 × 12-mark questions and 2 × 8-mark skills questions. It is a good idea to do the 20-mark question first so you don't run out of time at the end. Spend roughly about 45 minutes on this essay, 25 minutes each on the 12-mark responses and 20 minutes on the two skills questions. This equates to roughly 45 minutes per section.

Many candidates can describe and explain knowledge very well in the questions but there is a lack of discussion and analysis – see above.

Be specific

Candidates can lose out on marks because they just make very general statements without explaining more or quoting evidence to back things up – for example: 'poor people don't live as long'. This statement is very vague, is not well explained and has no statistics or evidence to back it up.

Refer to the question – make sure you answer it. If the question asks you 'To what extent does the media influence people to vote a certain way?' you must keep referring back to that – how much of an influence was that type of media in influencing the way that people vote?

It's good practice to write the question at the top of the question paper so you can see it as you write your essay.

The Assignment

This is worth 30 marks (one-third of the total marks) and is externally assessed. This means it is sent to the SQA to be marked. You will work on it throughout the year and it has to be written up under exam conditions. You will get 1 hour 30 mins to do this at a time decided by your teacher.

Structure and layout are important – the Assignment must be in the form of a report and is not a continuous essay. There's no one correct style to follow but the report must include all the information that you have decided to include. A suggested structure would be as follows:

*   Introduction – to include a detailed background to your issue (see below)
*   The options you have to decide between
*   Role and remit
*   Recommendation

- Arguments for recommendation
- Consideration of opposing arguments and rebuttal
- Conclusion
- Evaluation of sources

Mark allocation

1. Identifying and demonstrating knowledge and understanding of the issue about which a decision is to be made, including alternative courses of action. Candidates can be credited in a number of ways up to a maximum of 10 marks.

2. Analysing and synthesising information from a range of sources including use of specified resources. Candidates can be credited in a number of ways up to a maximum of 10 marks.

3. Evaluating the usefulness and reliability of a range of sources of information. Candidates can be credited in a number of ways up to a maximum of 2 marks.

4. Communicating information using the conventions of a report. Candidates can be credited in a number of ways up to a maximum of 4 marks.

5. Reaching a decision, supported by evidence, about the issue. Candidates can be credited in a number of ways up to a maximum of 4 marks.

Make sure you state your recommendation at the start of the report – this keeps you focused on what you are arguing for.

The resource sheet is two sides of A4 that show evidence of your research, which you can take in to the write-up. It is not a plan and if you set it out as such, you may lose marks from your structure allocation. You should refer to and use all the sources on the resource sheet but don't use sources that are not on the sheet. No marks will be given for straight copying from the source sheet.

You must source where your information has come from on your resource sheet. If using newspapers, state the publisher, date and headline. If using a website, make sure you give the publisher and date that the website was accessed on the resource sheet.

Pupils should use more technical language – Higher pupils should be able to do this, e.g. instead of 'poor areas', use 'areas of deprivation'.

Ten marks are allocated for knowledge. It is good practice to start with a detailed introduction that explains the issue fully and sets the background scene, politically, socially and perhaps internationally. This will enable you to pick up some good knowledge marks straight away.

You can refer to the same source more than once for different arguments and get credit for each reference.

Marks are given for evaluating your sources so be specific when you are evaluating them. Use words such as reliable, useful, bias, accurate and up-to-date.

Question Index

	Exam A	Exam B	Exam C
Section 1, Political Issues, 12-mark essay	✓	✗	✓
Section 1, Political Issues, 20-mark essay	✗	✓	✗
Section 1, Political Issues, Skills: objectivity	✓	✗	✗
Section 1, Political Issues, Skills: conclusions	✗	✗	✓
Section 2, Social Issues, 12-mark essay	✓	✓	✗
Section 2, Social Issues, 20-mark essay	✗	✗	✓
Section 2, Social issues, Skills: objectivity	✗	✓	✗
Section 2, Social Issues, Skills: conclusions	✓	✗	✗
Section 3, International Issues, 12-mark essay	✗	✓	✓
Section 3, International Issues, 20-mark essay	✓	✗	✗
Section 3, International Issues, Skills: objectivity	✗	✗	✓
Section 3, International Issues, Skills: conclusions	✗	✓	✗

Practice Exam A

MODERN STUDIES

Exam A

Duration — 2 hours 15 minutes

Total marks — 60

SECTION 1 — DEMOCRACY IN SCOTLAND AND THE UNITED KINGDOM — 20 marks

Attempt Question 1 and **EITHER** Question 2(a) **OR** 2(b)

SECTION 2 — SOCIAL ISSUES IN THE UNITED KINGDOM — 20 marks

Part A Social inequality in the United Kingdom

Part B Crime and the law in the United Kingdom

Attempt Question 3 and **EITHER** Question 4(a) **OR** 4(b) **OR** 4(c) **OR** 4(d)

SECTION 3 — INTERNATIONAL ISSUES — 20 marks

Part A World powers

Part B World issues

Attempt **EITHER** Question 5(a) **OR** 5(b) **OR** 5(c) **OR** 5(d)

In the answer booklet, you must clearly identify the question number you are attempting.

Use **blue** or **black** ink.

Leckie × Leckie

Scotland's leading educational publishers

SECTION 1 — DEMOCRACY IN SCOTLAND AND THE UNITED KINGDOM — 20 marks

Attempt Question 1 and **EITHER** Question 2(a) **OR** 2(b)

Question 1
Study Sources A and B then attempt the question that follows.

SOURCE A

SNP MPs Blast Old Fashioned Voting System in Westminster

New SNP parliamentarians have continued their criticism of House of Commons tradition – and they haven't held back. After five new Scottish MPs branded Prime Minister's Questions (PMQs) on Wednesday a "shambles", "a wall of infantile noise" and a "boys' club", there was fresh criticism on voting procedures. The Nationalists rubbished Westminster's "antiquated" voting system, asking why voting on bills could not be done electronically.

One of the aggrieved Scottish newbies, Dr Paul Monaghan claimed PMQs was "a spectacle for all the wrong reasons". He also vented frustration at the voting procedure in the Commons, whereby MPs have eight minutes to cast their ballot by physically walking through one of two doors, indicating whether they are in favour of or in disagreement with the motion.

"One of the challenges that I and my colleagues have to face is that we have to get from our offices to the voting lobby in eight minutes or else our representation is useless," he said. "It's not particularly suited to modern democracy – we all feel that it must be possible to vote electronically. We've all been given iPads so why could they not develop a simple app that would allow us to vote electronically and then carry on with our business?"

"The whole process takes about 20 minutes. We could have spent that time doing other things that would have been more for our constituents. There has to be a better way of doing things – it's these kinds of aspects of the UK Parliament that I think alienate the people of Scotland."

(continued)

Readers – have your say!

The whole political system needs to be brought into the 21st century. Westminster is being run for the sake of a rich political elite and it's time for the working class people of Britain to get their country back.
N. Pott
Chichester

Have you noticed though all the new boys and girls rail against tradition and as soon as it is changed the cost expands to fit the new modern style of doing things. If it isn't broke don't fix it – seen too many of these ideas of modernising mess everything up and cost the earth.
P. Barry
Essex

Once again, could not agree more with them. In today's world of technology, apps and wifi, 'walking through a door' while under the watchful eye of the party whips is hardly the best way to conduct democracy.
N. Holman
Derby

By all means, let them hide in their offices, not listen to debate and vote in a way no-one can track. Heaven forbid that they should actually have to sit in the chamber and publicly walk towards a door, in the sight of others, to cast their vote.
Z. Thruth
The Wirral

(Adapted from *The Huffington Post*, June 2015)

Section 1 Question 1 (continued)

SOURCE B

The House of Lords – Out of Date?

YouGov were commissioned by an organisation called Unlock Democracy to carry out an opinion poll asking people whether they felt that the House of Lords should be reformed. Currently the House of Lords acts as a check on the House of Commons and can revise and delay laws. Lords – called peers – are currently all appointed by the government apart from a minority that have inherited their title.

Some participants in the survey believe that the current system is undemocratic – anyone involved in making laws should have some kind of accountability through elections. Some people suggested that many felt that current peers were out of touch with modern life and in need of an update.

The main difference between survey participants who thought the House of Lords should be fully or partially elected rested on the role of specialist members with experience in certain fields – who might not be included in a fully elected house. Lord Alan Sugar is probably the most famous example of this type of experience, being a successful businessman.

In comparison, those participants who argued the House of Lords should remain as it is pointed out that the current system is beneficial, in that it isn't necessarily involved with party politics, meaning that laws can be scrutinised impartially and without the drama of the Commons – and for the wealth of experience held by specialised, appointed members.

What should the House of Lords look like?

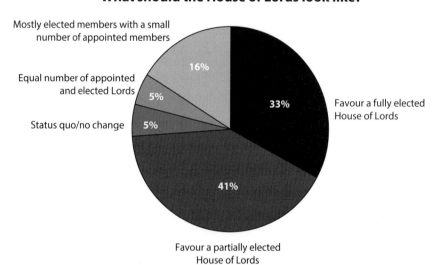

- Mostly elected members with a small number of appointed members — 16%
- Equal number of appointed and elected Lords — 5%
- Status quo/no change — 5%
- Favour a fully elected House of Lords — 33%
- Favour a partially elected House of Lords — 41%

YouGov interviewed 2349 adults online between the 18th and 20th of April 2012. The figures were weighted as representative of all British adults aged over 18.

Attempt the following question, using only the information in Sources A and B above.

To what extent is it accurate to state that there is a clear desire to modernise the system of law-making in Westminster?

In your answer you may wish to evaluate the reliability of the sources.

8

Section 1 (continued)

Attempt **EITHER** Question 2(a) **OR** 2(b)

Question 2

(a) | *The media has been a major influence on the way that people vote in recent elections.* |

Evaluate the importance of the media in influencing the way people vote.

You should refer to elections and types of media in Scotland **or** the United Kingdom **or** both in your answer.

12

OR

(b) | *Parliamentary representatives have many pressures on them when doing their job.* |

Evaluate the importance of the different factors which parliamentary representatives have to consider when carrying out their duties, both in and out of parliament.

You should refer to parliamentary representatives in Scotland **or** the United Kingdom **or** both in your answer.

12

SECTION 2 — SOCIAL ISSUES IN THE UNITED KINGDOM — 20 marks

Attempt Question 3 and **EITHER** Question 4(a) **OR** 4(b) **OR** 4(c) **OR** 4(d)

Question 3

Study Sources A, B and C then attempt the question which follows.

SOURCE A

Gender Inequality in the Workplace

David Cameron has said on gender equality "there has been a recent slew of good news". But the reality is somewhat different. Let's start with the fact that, in the last ten years, the number of women forced out of their jobs – either when they become pregnant or on their return to work after giving birth – has almost doubled.

With its rather clunky title, "Pregnancy and Maternity-Related Discrimination and Disadvantage", a recent paper included some shocking findings. Interviews with more than 3200 women about their experiences of being pregnant at work, or returning to their jobs after giving birth, found that 11% reported having been dismissed, forced to take redundancy or treated so badly that they felt they had no choice but to resign.

According to the Equality and Human Rights Commission, which co-commissioned the research, assuming that these trends are replicated across the entire workforce means that as many as 54,000 new mothers in the UK may be forced out of their jobs each year.

But what few seemed to notice was that the new figures showed we are moving in the exact opposite direction of progress. 10 years ago, the Equal Opportunities Commission produced a similar report on maternity rights in the workplace, with the much more snappy title of "Greater Expectations". That report estimated that the number of pregnant women and new mums forced out of their jobs was around 30,000 each year. Ten years on, the number is close to twice that.

If the new report achieves anything it's to remind us of just how much further women still have to go before reaching genuine equality in the workplace. Last week's report can ultimately have a positive effect if it inspires more women to take up the challenge to stand up to discrimination wherever we see it. So let's organise. Let's put a stop to it!

Section 2 Question 3 (continued)

SOURCE B

Widening Gender Gap

The evidence in the new report from the World Economic Forum is very plain indeed. In Britain, the gender gap between men and women is stuck or widening. As a consequence, the UK is heading down the gender equality league table, as other countries do more and give higher priority to reversing their own inequalities. It is only eight years since the WEF began conducting this annual survey. In that short time, however, Britain has gone from ninth in the world in 2006 to 26th this year.

That is not the same thing as saying that everything about the gender gap in Britain is getting worse. The UK's level of equality in economic participation has improved slightly since 2006, while the educational equality level remains broadly constant, whilst things have got slightly worse in health and in politics. What is striking, though, is that if things merely remain the same they lead to a comparative decline, while others do better. The five Nordic countries – Iceland, Finland, Norway, Sweden and Denmark – have all made big improvements in most of the categories while Britain has stalled and been overtaken.

There have been improvements in recent years. The world is moving in a more gender-equal direction, based on these measures. But the progress remains too slow. At the current rate, it will be 2095 before the world's pay gap at work and equality gap in management are eliminated. That is 81 years away. That is still true in 2014. Even today, we have a lot to learn and to do.

Factfile

- The full-time gender pay gap is 10%, and the average part-time pay gap is 34.5%.

- It is estimated that for each year a mother is absent from the workplace her future wages will reduce by 5%.

- Approximately 70% of people in national minimum wage jobs are women.

- 54% of women working part-time have been found to be 'employed below their potential', i.e. doing work for which they are over-qualified, which amounts to 2.8 million women.

- A study by the Fawcett Society found that 51% of women and men from middle management to director level identify stereotyping as the major hurdle facing women at work.

- There is a large discrepancy in leave entitlements between mothers and their partners: mothers can take 39 weeks of paid maternity leave whilst fathers/partners can only take 2 weeks of paid leave. Compare this to Scandinavian countries such as Sweden where leave is shared between the father and mother and can be up to 60 weeks.

- Up to 60,000 women are sacked each year simply for being pregnant and each year an estimated 440,000 women lose out on pay rises or promotions as a result of pregnancy.

Section 2 Question 3 (continued)

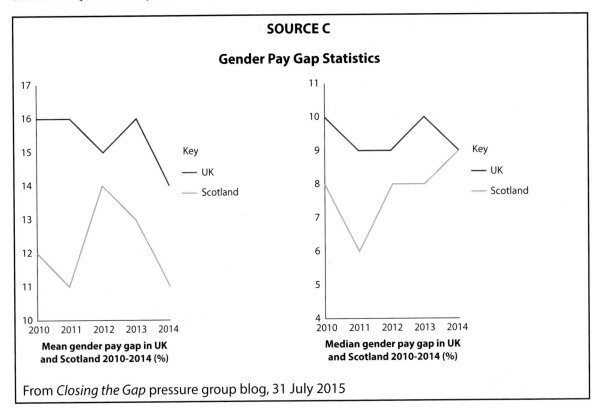

SOURCE C

Gender Pay Gap Statistics

Mean gender pay gap in UK and Scotland 2010-2014 (%)

Median gender pay gap in UK and Scotland 2010-2014 (%)

Key — UK — Scotland

From *Closing the Gap* pressure group blog, 31 July 2015

Attempt the following question, using only the information in Sources A, B and C above.

What conclusions can be drawn about gender equality in the UK?

You must draw conclusions about:

• the effects of having children on female employment

• the gender pay gap

You must give an overall conclusion about gender inequality in the workplace in the UK.

8

Section 2 (continued)

Attempt **EITHER** Question 4(a) **OR** 4(b) **OR** 4(c) **OR** 4(d)

Question 4

Part A: Social inequality in the United Kingdom

Answers may refer to Scotland **or** the United Kingdom **or** both.

(a) Analyse the success of government policies in tackling income inequality.   **12**

OR

(b) Analyse the reasons why health inequalities continue to exist.   **12**

OR

Part B: Crime and the law in the United Kingdom

Answers may refer to Scotland **or** the United Kingdom **or** both.

(c) Analyse the success of government policies in tackling crime.   **12**

OR

(d) Analyse the ways in which offenders and their families are affected.   **12**

SECTION 3 — INTERNATIONAL ISSUES — 20 marks

Attempt **EITHER** Question 5(a) **OR** 5(b) **OR** 5(c) **OR** 5(d)

Question 5

Part A: World powers

With reference to a world power you have studied:

(a) | *The constitutional arrangements and institutions of a country should ensure that no branch of government has too much power.*

Discuss.   **20**

OR

(b) To what extent does this world power have an influence over other world powers?   **20**

OR

Part B: World issues

With reference to a world issue you have studied:

(c) Discuss whether international organisations have made significant progress in resolving this world issue.   **20**

OR

(d) To what extent has this world issue had an impact on the international community?   **20**

[END OF PRACTICE QUESTION PAPER]

MODERN STUDIES

Exam B

Duration — 2 hours 15 minutes

Total marks — 60

SECTION 1 — DEMOCRACY IN SCOTLAND AND THE UNITED KINGDOM — 20 marks

Attempt Question 1(a) **OR** 1(b)

SECTION 2 — SOCIAL ISSUES IN THE UNITED KINGDOM — 20 marks

      Part A Social inequality in the United Kingdom

      Part B Crime and the law in the United Kingdom

Attempt Question 2 and **EITHER** Question 3(a) **OR** 3(b) **OR** 3(c) **OR** 3(d)

SECTION 3 — INTERNATIONAL ISSUES — 20 marks

      Part A World powers

      Part B World issues

Attempt Question 4 and **EITHER** Question 5(a) **OR** 5(b) **OR** 5(c) **OR** 5(d)

In the answer booklet, you must clearly identify the question number you are attempting.

Use **blue** or **black** ink.

Leckie×Leckie

Scotland's leading educational publishers

MARKS

SECTION 1 — DEMOCRACY IN SCOTLAND AND THE UNITED KINGDOM — 20 marks

Attempt **EITHER** Question 1(a) **OR** 1(b)

Question 1

(a) | *There are many factors that affect the way that people vote or indeed, if they vote.* |

Discuss.

You should refer to different factors in Scotland **or** the United Kingdom **or** both in your answer.　　　　**20**

OR

(b) | *People can participate in, and influence the political process in many different ways.* |

Discuss.

To what extent can people participate in and influence the political system?

You should refer to examples of participation in Scotland **or** the United Kingdom **or** both in your answer.　　　　**20**

SECTION 2 — SOCIAL ISSUES IN THE UNITED KINGDOM — 20 marks

Attempt Question 2 and **EITHER** Question 3(a) **OR** 3(b) **OR** 3(c) **OR** 3(d)

Question 2

Study Sources A, B and C then attempt the question which follows.

SOURCE A

Department of Education – Factfile
Holidays in term-time

You must make sure your child gets a full-time education that meets their needs (e.g. if they have special educational needs). You have to get permission from the head teacher if you want to take your child out of school during term time. You can only do this if:

- you make an application to the head teacher in advance (from the parent the child normally lives with)

- there are exceptional circumstances

It's up to the head teacher how many days your child can be away from school if leave is granted. You can be fined for taking your child on holiday during term time without the school's permission.

Legal action to enforce school attendance could be:

- **A penalty notice.** The penalty is £60, rising to £120 if paid after 21 days but within 28 days. If you don't pay the fine you may be prosecuted.

- **Prosecution.** You could get a fine of up to £2,500, a community order or a jail sentence up to 3 months. The court also gives you a Parenting Order.

Section 2 Question 2 (continued)

SOURCE B

Viewpoints

Pretty much every summer as far back as they can remember, we've set off on an expedition so that we can get our kids amazing experiences. The trips have been seven weeks long (as short a time as we could manage to whip around our chosen destinations and still get a proper flavour for them).

Now the new rules could change all this. Don't get us wrong, we understand the importance of school attendance but it seems parents of children who religiously turn up for classes five days every week each and every term are being penalised for the poor attendance of others.

Of course three weeks off mid-Christmas term would be harmful (not to mention, create additional work for hard-pressed teachers who would have to help them catch up on their return) but it's hard to see the harm in a week off at the end of summer term. There's no tests and our kids are 9 and 6 – not exam age.

Being young and impressionable we believe the experiences we're providing don't just create wonderful family memories as important as they are, but help develop outside interests. Life shouldn't all be about exam results after all. Last year our timid daughter surprised us in Italy by climbing with a guide up a 60 foot vertical rock-face. As Charlie jumped joyously into the car as we raced for the ferry last July, I asked what he'd done at school that day. He replied: "We practised for sports day and watched a DVD".
Ben Thurbeck, travel writer, London

Why shouldn't you take your children out of school during term-time? Even just a day or two early? After all, wouldn't it be great to give them the family holiday of a lifetime? This is the argument most often used by parents who yank their children out of school ahead of half-term, or pop them back in a few days late. After all, they are my child, and I should choose what they do... right? And at half-term, the prices of holidays spike.

Well, yes, it's your child. But school isn't day care. It's an educational institution that employs professionals who rely on having a strong, supportive community. Removing them from school during term-time sends a message to the school community and, more importantly, to your child, that you don't take their education very seriously. Taking a child on holiday when school is in session is disruptive for the child and the entire class, because the child will have to catch up when they return.

Denham Kite, a head teacher in Hull, said he had sympathy for parents but absences could not be approved just to save money on holidays. "They are things we have to plan for and there will be members of staff in the same situation," he said. "We do want to make sure that children come to school. They don't have their education disrupted or the education of others in the classroom when they come back and try to get them up to speed with other children."
Sally Cooper

(Adapted from *Telegraph Travel* article, 5 September 2015)

Section 2 Question 2 (continued)

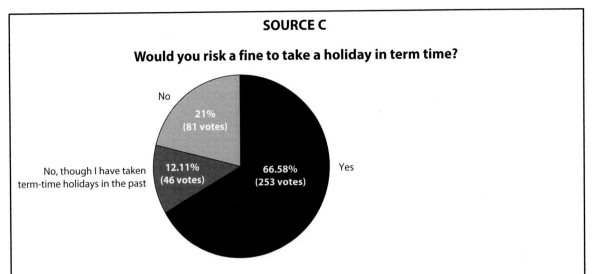

SOURCE C

Would you risk a fine to take a holiday in term time?

No — 21% (81 votes)

No, though I have taken term-time holidays in the past — 12.11% (46 votes)

66.58% (253 votes) — Yes

(Adapted from *Telegraph Travel* article, 5 September 2015)

Number of fines issued by two selected councils to parents for term time holidays

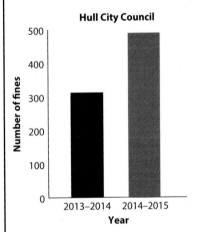

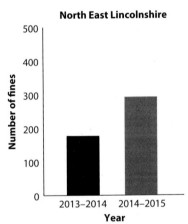

(BBC Humberside, 10 April 2015)

PETITION AGAINST FINES FOR TERM-TIME HOLIDAYS

'*Reverse the amendments to the term time family holiday rules under The Education (Pupil Registration) (England) Regulations 2006 which came into force on 1 September 2013.*'

227,961 signatures reached as of 5 September 2015

(38 Degrees website)

Attempt the following question, using only the information in sources A, B and C above.

To what extent is it accurate to state that taking children out of school in term time is wrong and damages their education?

In your answer you may wish to evaluate the reliability of the sources.

8

Section 2 (continued)

Attempt **EITHER** Question 3(a) **OR** 3(b) **OR** 3(c) **OR** 3(d)

Question 3

Part A: Social inequality in the United Kingdom

Answers may refer to Scotland **or** the United Kingdom **or** both.

(a)   Evaluate the different theories that best explain one inequality of your choice.   **12**

OR

(b)   Evaluate the success of government policies to reduce inequality.   **12**

OR

Part B: Crime and the law in the United Kingdom

Answers may refer to Scotland **or** the United Kingdom **or** both.

(c)   Evaluate the different theories that best explain the causes of crime.   **12**

OR

(d)   Evaluate the success of different approaches to solve crime.   **12**

SECTION 3 — INTERNATIONAL ISSUES — 20 marks

Attempt Question 4 and **EITHER** Question 5(a) **OR** 5(b) **OR** 5(c) **OR** 5(d)

Question 4

Study sources A, B and C then attempt the question which follows.

SOURCE A

The Immigration Debate – View of Nigel Farage

The results of the Ipsos Mori poll are astounding – yet unsurprising. They describe the real concern that the majority of British people have for uncontrolled immigration: half of the respondents rank it as one of their biggest worries, compared with just over a quarter who said their greatest fear was the economy.

I still find it astonishing that we live in an age where the two biggest parties share the same policy on the defining issue of the time – they are both committed to open borders with the European Union. You only have to look at the numbers to see the truth: in the 12 months to June 2005 under Tony Blair, net migration was at 320,000. Under David Cameron's premiership, net migration to Britain was an estimated 330,000 in the year to March 2015 – the highest figure on record. Different parties: same undesirable outcome.

Mass immigration on this scale has never been something the British people wanted nor asked for. Part of the problem is that the numbers in which people are arriving has made integration virtually impossible with huge pressure being placed on public services. Two in five council areas in England now admit that they will not have enough primary school places by September 2016. The housing market has seen the effects too – just to keep up with current population surges, a new house would have to be built every seven minutes.

This isn't just about what's going on in the UK though. I believe that the reason immigration is more of a concern than ever before for the British people relates to what we see going on beyond our shores. We see the chaos in Calais and in the Mediterranean where thousands of migrants are risking their lives. We see that the issue of open borders and mass immigration is no longer simply an issue of social problems and the impact on British workers, it is fast becoming one of national security. It is clear that in the forthcoming EU referendum the issue of border controls will dominate the debate. Particularly since the EU's Common Asylum Policy has relaxed its criteria, allowing pretty much anyone who comes to Europe to stay.

Now we are seeing the effects: Greece is in a state of chaos unable to cope, with a staggering 124,000 migrants arriving via boat this year alone, a 750 per cent increase from the same period the year before. Germany meanwhile is revising its numbers upwards on an almost daily basis. The latest figure they are citing is of 800,000 asylum seekers and refugees entering their country this year alone.

I believe that the British people have seen quite enough. I believe that they want an Australian-style immigration policy that allocates work permits to those our economy needs, that says no to those whose skills we do not need, and that gives an emphatic denial of entry to those we have any suspicion want to do us harm.

Section 3 Question 4 (continued)

SOURCE B

Office of National Statistics (ONS) statistics on UK immigration, August 2015

Net migration

Net migration is the net total of migrants during the period, that is, the total number of immigrants less the annual number of emigrants.

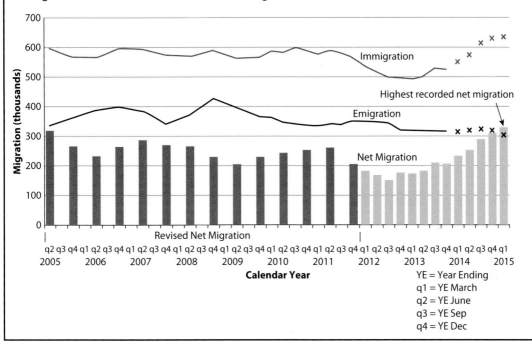

Section 3 Question 4 (continued)

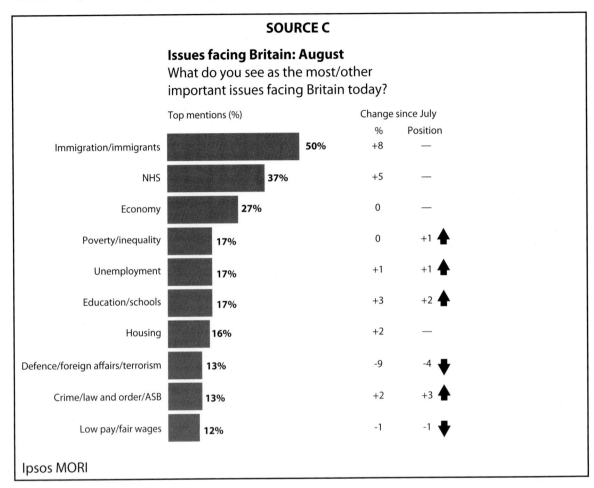

SOURCE C

Issues facing Britain: August
What do you see as the most/other important issues facing Britain today?

Top mentions (%)

Change since July

	Top mentions (%)	%	Position
Immigration/immigrants	50%	+8	—
NHS	37%	+5	—
Economy	27%	0	—
Poverty/inequality	17%	0	+1 ⬆
Unemployment	17%	+1	+1 ⬆
Education/schools	17%	+3	+2 ⬆
Housing	16%	+2	—
Defence/foreign affairs/terrorism	13%	-9	-4 ⬇
Crime/law and order/ASB	13%	+2	+3 ⬆
Low pay/fair wages	12%	-1	-1 ⬇

Ipsos MORI

Attempt the following question, using only the information in Sources A, B and C above.

What conclusions can be drawn about immigration in the EU?

You must draw conclusions about:

• the level of immigration

• public attitudes to immigration in the UK

You must give an overall conclusion about the impact of immigration.

8

Section 3 (continued)

Attempt **EITHER** Question 5(a) **OR** 5(b) **OR** 5(c) **OR** 5(d)

Question 5

Part A: World powers

With reference to a world power you have studied:

(a)   Analyse the impact of a socio-economic issue on the citizens of this world power.   **12**

OR

(b)   Analyse the ways citizens can have their views represented within the political system.   **12**

OR

Part B: World issues

With reference to a world issue you have studied:

(c)   Analyse the main causes of this world issue.   **12**

OR

(d)   Analyse the role of national governments in trying to resolve this issue.   **12**

[END OF PRACTICE QUESTION PAPER]

Practice Exam C

MODERN STUDIES

Exam C

Duration — 2 hours 15 minutes

Total marks — 60

SECTION 1 — DEMOCRACY IN SCOTLAND AND THE UNITED KINGDOM — 20 marks

Attempt Question 1 and **EITHER** Question 2(a) **OR** 2(b)

SECTION 2 — SOCIAL ISSUES IN THE UNITED KINGDOM — 20 marks

      Part A Social inequality in the United Kingdom

      Part B Crime and the law in the United Kingdom

Attempt Question 3(a) **OR** 3(b) **OR** 3(c) **OR** 3(d)

SECTION 3 — INTERNATIONAL ISSUES — 20 marks

      Part A World powers

      Part B World issues

Attempt Question 4 and **EITHER** Question 5(a) **OR** 5(b) **OR** 5(c) **OR** 5(d)

In the answer booklet, you must clearly identify the question number you are attempting.

Use **blue** or **black** ink.

Leckie ✕ Leckie

Scotland's leading educational publishers

SECTION 1 — DEMOCRACY IN SCOTLAND AND THE UNITED KINGDOM — 20 marks

Attempt Question 1 and **EITHER** Question 2(a) **OR** 2(b)

Question 1

Study Sources A, B and C then attempt the question which follows.

SOURCE A

The TV Debate 2 April 2015

The General Election Campaign 2015: Who's Winning?

Following on from the success of the Prime Ministerial debates from the General Election campaign 2010, all 7 party leaders whose parties can win seats in the forthcoming election took part in a TV debate on 2 April 2015. It was broadcast on ITV and was watched by 7.4 million viewers.

The leader of the SNP, Nicola Sturgeon, was hailed in Scotland for her assured performance and suddenly found herself on the national stage. Despite warnings from the Conservative and Labour parties on the effects of voting SNP, political enemies admitted that she was the biggest winner in the TV debate. She even had to fend off questions from the media asking if the SNP was going to field candidates in English seats saying, 'I think it is a reflection of how out of touch the whole Westminster system has become'.

Labour pointed out that Ed Miliband got higher ratings in 3 out of 4 polls taken after the debate than the SNP. But Labour MP Diane Abbott said: 'Good to see Nicola Sturgeon taking Nigel Farage to task on immigration.'

Throughout the TV debates and the campaign, Nicola Sturgeon has said the SNP would back Labour in a minority government but it would not be a formal coalition, which happened with the Conservatives and LibDems in 2010. The SNP would vote with Labour to keep it in government but would want some things in return such as increased spending on public services as well as an end to the Trident nuclear submarine. Labour leader Ed Miliband has also ruled out a formal coalition with the SNP.

Many opinion polls and surveys put SNP gaining 50% of the vote and even the Tories beating the Labour party in Scotland. However, according to *New Statesman* research, these figures are stark and risk some SNP supporters being too complacent and possibly not turning out. Based on their averaged figures, the SNP look to be far ahead of Labour and all others, but have far more often been around 40, rather than 50 per cent. And Labour, despite their relative collapse since 2010, are still half a dozen points or so ahead of the Tories in Scotland.

But the consequences for Labour and the election could still be dramatic – a lot depends on the SNP vote holding up.

Section 1 Question 1 (continued)

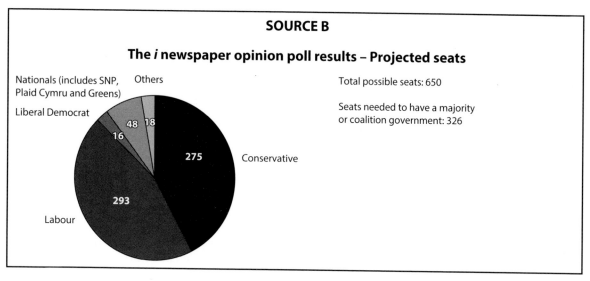

SOURCE B

The _i_ newspaper opinion poll results – Projected seats

Nationals (includes SNP, Plaid Cymru and Greens)

Others

Liberal Democrat

48 18

16

275 Conservative

293

Labour

Total possible seats: 650

Seats needed to have a majority or coalition government: 326

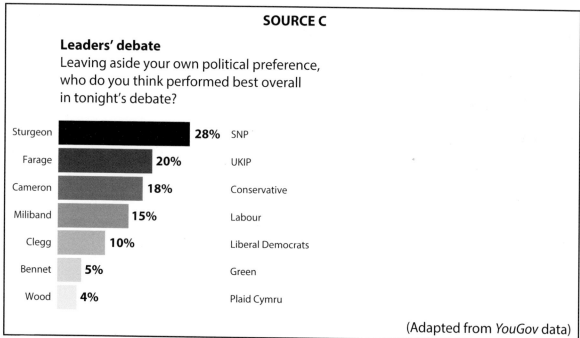

SOURCE C

Leaders' debate

Leaving aside your own political preference, who do you think performed best overall in tonight's debate?

Leader	Result	Party
Sturgeon	28%	SNP
Farage	20%	UKIP
Cameron	18%	Conservative
Miliband	15%	Labour
Clegg	10%	Liberal Democrats
Bennet	5%	Green
Wood	4%	Plaid Cymru

(Adapted from _YouGov_ data)

Attempt the following question, using only the information in Sources A, B and C above.

What conclusions can be drawn about the 2015 General Election campaign after the party leaders' TV debate?

You must draw conclusions about:

• the party leaders who performed the best in the debate

• the party/parties thought likely at the time to form the government after the election

You must give an overall conclusion about who performed the best in the election campaign.

8

Section 1 (continued)

Attempt **EITHER** Question 2(a) **OR** 2(b)

Question 2

(a)

> *There is an increasing call for the system of choosing political representatives to be changed.*

Evaluate the view that current electoral systems used to elect representatives should be changed.

You should refer to electoral systems in Scotland **or** the United Kingdom **or** both in your answer.

12

OR

(b)

> *There is an increasing call for the Scottish Government to be given more powers to govern Scotland.*

Evaluate the view that the Scottish Parliament needs more powers from the UK Parliament to govern Scotland.

You may refer to parliamentary powers in Scotland **or** the United Kingdom **or** both in your answer.

12

SECTION 2 — SOCIAL ISSUES IN THE UNITED KINGDOM — 20 marks

Attempt **EITHER** Question 3(a) **OR** 3(b) **OR** 3(c) **OR** 3(d)

Question 3

Part A: Social inequality in the United Kingdom

Answers may refer to Scotland **or** the United Kingdom **or** both.

(a) | *The government has a major responsibility to try to close the inequality gap.* |

To what extent is it the responsibility of the government to deal with inequalities? **20**

OR

(b) | *Income and wealth inequality has a major impact on people in society.* |

Discuss the impact of income inequality on a group in society you have studied. **20**

OR

Part B: Crime and the law in the United Kingdom

Answers may refer to Scotland **or** the United Kingdom **or** both.

(c) | *Crime can be explained by sociological and individualist theories.* |

To what extent are social explanations of crime more valid than individualist theories of crime? **20**

OR

(d) | *Crime has a major impact on individuals, their families and the wider community.* |

Discuss the social, economic and political impact of crime. **20**

SECTION 3 — INTERNATIONAL ISSUES — 20 marks

Attempt Question 4 and **EITHER** Question 5(a) **OR** 5(b) **OR** 5(c) **OR** 5(d)

Question 4

Study Sources A, B and C then attempt the question which follows.

SOURCE A

Inequality between Men and Women in the European Union

A key aim of the European Union is to bring about equality between men and women in all aspects of life including health, education and in the workplace. According to the Global Gender Gap Report, some EU countries are amongst the most equal in the world with Germany in 11th place out of 134. Some of the newer countries do less well with the Czech Republic in 75th place and Estonia at 52nd place. There has been considerable progress over the years but more has to be done as inequalities still exist especially in newer member states.

Although women usually live longer than men, the EU is concerned with men's health as much as that of women's. Although average life expectancy and quality of life have increased over the last sixty years, there are still differences between countries. Certain diseases affect men more than women. Smoking is more common among men than women in all EU countries and this has an impact on diseases such as strokes, cancer and heart disease.

There has been an increase in unemployment across the EU and this has affected men more than women in some countries. When it comes to pay, women still earn less than men in every single member state of the EU although the gender pay gap is narrower in some countries compared to others. Many women are employed in part-time work and this tends to bring the average wage down. In professional occupations, women are making some progress but still lag behind men especially at boardroom level.

In education, within the EU, females tend to outnumber males at college or university and in the future this may result in the gender pay gap decreasing and more women ending up in better paid jobs. In all EU states literacy rates are very similar for males and females.

(Adapted from an article in the *Independent* newspaper)

Section 3 Question 4 (continued)

SOURCE B

**Information on Health and Life Expectancy from
Selected European Countries for Men and Women**

Deaths per 100,000 resulting from diseases linked to smoking

	Lung cancer		Heart disease		Stroke	
	Male	Female	Male	Female	Male	Female
France	48	15	55	21	34	24
Czech Republic	53	16	228	137	87	71
Germany	42	16	117	62	42	36
Estonia	51	9	330	163	97	63

Life expectancy

	Male	Female
France	77.4	84.4
Czech Republic	73.4	79.8
Germany	77.3	82.1
Estonia	67.3	78.5

Section 3 Question 4 (continued)

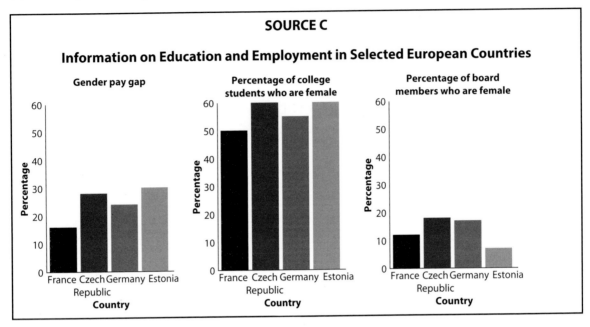

SOURCE C

Information on Education and Employment in Selected European Countries

Attempt the following question, using only the information in Sources A, B and C above.

To what extent is it accurate to state that social and economic inequalities exist equally in all areas of the EU?

In your answer you may wish to evaluate the reliability of the sources.

8

Section 3 (continued)

Attempt **EITHER** Question 5(a) **OR** 5(b) **OR** 5(c) **OR** 5(d)

Question 5

Part A: World powers

With reference to a world power you have studied:

(a) Analyse its influence on world affairs by its involvement in international organisations.   **12**

OR

(b) Analyse the nature and extent of socio-economic inequality.   **12**

OR

Part B: World issues

With reference to a world issue you have studied:

(c) Analyse the nature and extent of this issue.   **12**

OR

(d) Analyse the effects this issue has had on individuals.   **12**

[END OF PRACTICE QUESTION PAPER]

Marking instructions

Mark Scheme for Exam A

Section 1: Democracy in Scotland and the UK

Question	General marking instructions for this type of question	Max. mark	Specific marking instructions for this question
1	The candidate is required to interpret/evaluate up to three complex sources of information detecting and explaining the extent of objectivity. In order to achieve credit candidates must show evidence which supports the extent of accuracy in a given viewpoint. • Award up to 3 marks for appropriate use of evidence depending on the quality of the explanation and the synthesis of the evidence for one explanation of the extent of objectivity. • For full marks, candidates must refer to all sources in their answer. • For full marks candidates must make an overall judgement as to the extent of the accuracy of the given statement. • Maximum of 6 marks if no overall judgement made on extent of accuracy of the statement.	8	'There is a clear desire to modernise the system of law-making in Westminster.' Candidates can be credited in a number of ways up to a maximum of 8 marks. **Evidence that supports the view:** • Source A – a number of new MPs have criticised the voting system in the House of Commons as a 'shambles', 'antiquated', 'boys' club'. • Source A – call for a more electronic voting system as all MPs have iPads which would be more efficient than walking through a door. • Source A – voting takes up to 20 minutes and that time could be spent on helping constituents. • Source A – there are only 8 minutes to get to the debating chamber to vote. • Source A – backed up by comments from the political blog – N. Pott and N. Holman. • Source B – call for Lords to be held accountable through elections. • Source B – call for Lords to be more up to date. • Source B – pie chart showing that only 5% favour the current system of the House of Lords. • Source B – largest percentage favour a partially elected House of Lords.

Possible responses:

Source A shows that many new MPs find Prime Minster questions (PMQs) a bit of a joke calling it a shambles due to the fact that it resembles a 'boys' club' and a wall of infantile noise. There are calls for the voting system to be changed from having to physically walk through doors to using the iPads that all MPs have been issued with. **(1 mark, relevant evidence)** *Source B shows that many felt that there should be House of Lords reform as they felt it was out of touch and needed an update. This is backed up by the pie chart: the biggest percentages in the survey showed that most people wanted either a partial or fully elected House of Lords at 41% and 33% respectively, therefore showing a clear desire to modernise the system of law making in Scotland.* **(3 marks, evidence synthesised from within a source with evaluative comment)**

Evidence that does not support the view:

- Source A – voting procedure is historic and has worked for centuries – backed up by the political blog and the viewpoint of P. Barry.

- Source A – this is only the view of the 50 SNP MPs – we are not told the views of the 600 other MPs.

- Source A – some people might argue that 20 minutes isn't a long period of time to make key decisions.

- Source A – modernising may cost money, especially if IT is used – P. Barry viewpoint.

- Source A – making MPs walk through the door to vote is a way of ensuring that they have listened to the debate as opposed to hiding in their offices.

- Source B – people who supported the House of Lords argued there is a wealth of experience from those peers that have key experience in their previous work, e.g. Lord Alan Sugar.

- Candidates may be awarded up to a maximum of 2 marks for incorporating an evaluation of the reliability of the sources in their explanations, although this is not mandatory.

- Source B – people who support the status quo argue that the current system allows decisions to be made on laws impartially.

Possible responses:

From Source B, it is argued that the House of Lords is fine as it is; it plays a key role in scrutinising bills without party politics being involved and by experienced people with a wealth of knowledge. **(1 mark, relevant knowledge)** *Views from the newspaper blog show that being seen to walk through the voting doors shows the MP has taken part and listened to debates as opposed to just voting with an app. This shows there is not a clear desire to modernise the system of law-making and some people are happy with the current system.* **(2 marks, relevant knowledge and evaluative comment)**

Candidates may also be credited up to 2 marks on any comment/ evaluation of the origin and reliability of the sources:

The Huffington Post calls itself an internet newspaper of blogs, news and video but often is referred to as a hate site where its one-sided news cannot be trusted – it is thought to be extremely biased and left wing. Also, as this article is 'adapted' it may be less reliable than when it was originally written. **(2 marks)**

YouGov is a well-known worldwide provider of opinion polls. For this poll, 2349 people were polled in an online survey, which is a good sample size and reflects accurately the views of people over 18, therefore it is a reliable source. **(2 marks)**

For full marks, candidates must make an overall judgement as to the extent of the accuracy of the given statement:

Overall, the evidence does support the view, as the voting system in the House of Commons is the same one that has been used for hundreds of years and is struggling to survive in a world where IT is used. Reform of the House of Lords is clearly required as only 5% of those asked in a YouGov poll thought the status quo should remain. **(2 marks)**

2a	12		

Evaluate the importance of the media in influencing the way people vote.

Candidates can be credited in a number of ways up to a maximum of 12 marks.

Credit reference to aspects of the following:

- Traditional media – press, TV, radio.
- New media – the influence of social media, e.g. Facebook, Twitter.
- Party political websites.
- Online forums.
- Opinion polls.
- Link media to other factors on voting, e.g. social class.

Any other valid point that meets the criteria described in the general marking principles for this type of question.

Possible approaches to answering the question:

Most people rely on traditional forms of media for information about elections. BBC television has to be neutral as it is publicly funded and other TV channels follow suit. Therefore it is more likely to be a source of information about the political parties and the election rather than an influence on voting. **(1 mark, analysis)**

The Sun newspaper is the biggest selling tabloid – it has always claimed credit for backing the winner of elections. In 2010 and 2015, they backed the Conservatives and they won both claiming 'it was The Sun wot won it'. However, in the Scottish Parliament elections in 2007, the Scottish Sun backed Labour and ran anti-SNP front pages. However, the SNP went on to win the election and run Scotland with a minority government. In this instance, the press coverage did not sway voters to vote a certain way – other factors were at play. **(3 marks, KU and analysis)**

Evaluation involves making a judgement(s) based on criteria, drawing conclusions on the extent to which a view is supported by the evidence; the overall counter-arguments including possible alternative interpretations; the overall impact/significance of the factors when taken together; the relative importance of factors in relation to the context.

Credit responses that make reference to:

- Different types of media used in election campaigns.
- The extent to which they influence the way people vote.

Up to 8 marks for KU (description, explanation and exemplification) and up to 4 marks for evaluative comments.

Award up to 6 marks per point. Candidates should be credited up to full marks if they answer within a Scottish context only, a UK context only or refer to both Scotland and the UK.

Where a candidate makes more evaluative points than are required to gain the maximum allocation of 4 marks, these can be credited as knowledge and understanding marks provided they meet the criteria for this.

12	In the 2010 election campaign TV debates were held for the first time. The three candidates for Prime Minister from the main UK parties took part in three televised election debates which attracted a large audience, at times 10 million. **(1 mark, KU)** Nick Clegg, leader of the Liberal Democrats at that time, was thought to have performed well as shown by the catchphrase 'I agree with Nick'. **(1 mark, analysis)** However, the result of the 2010 election showed that the Lib Dems only increased their vote by 1%. **(1 mark, analysis)** This TV debate, although showing increased levels of interest in the election contest and increased support for Nick Clegg resulted in a minimal increase in votes for the Lib Dems. **(1 mark, evaluative comment)** This may have been due to the FPTP electoral system as many felt their vote would have been wasted if they had voted Lib Dem. **(1 mark, analysis)** **(5 marks, knowledge with analysis and evaluative comment)** Evaluate the importance of the different factors that parliamentary representatives have to consider when carrying out their duties, both in and out of parliament. Candidates can be credited in a number of ways up to a maximum of 12 marks. **Credit reference to aspects of the following:** • Constituency support • Political party manifestos • Role and power of the whips • Patronage and power of the First/Prime Minister • Conscience Any other valid point that meets the criteria described in the general marking principles for this type of question.
2b	Evaluation involves making a judgement(s) based on criteria, drawing conclusions on the extent to which a view is supported by the evidence; counter-arguments including possible alternative interpretations; the overall impact/significance of the factors when taken together; the relative importance of factors in relation to the context. **Credit responses that make reference to:** • The different pressures MSPs face when doing their job. • An evaluation of the amount of pressure.

Up to 8 marks for KU (description, explanation and exemplification) and up to 4 marks for evaluative comments.

Award up to 6 marks per point. Candidates should be credited up to full marks if they answer within a Scottish context only, a UK context only or refer to both Scotland and the UK.

Where a candidate makes more evaluative points than are required to gain the maximum allocation of 4 marks, these can be credited as knowledge and understanding marks provided they meet the criteria for this.

Possible approaches to answering the question (Scottish dimension):

MSPs have to weigh up the needs of their constituents with the needs of the political party to which they belong. During election time the party provides a campaign team to distribute election materials and drum up support for the candidate. In return, once elected, the MSP must carry out the promises made in the election manifesto and support the party when required. **(2 marks, 1 knowledge and 1 analysis)** *One exception to this is in matters of conscience. In the vote in Parliament for the Assisted Suicide Bill, MSPs were allowed a free vote based on their own values and beliefs as opposed to having to listen to constituents or toe the party line. This shows that, although MSPs have to toe the party line for most political votes, there is some scope for free votes.* **(4 marks, 2 KU and 2 evaluative statement)**

Possible approaches to answering the question (UK dimension):

MPs have to balance the wishes of the constituents with the demands of the parliamentary party. Parties appoint a Chief Whip whose job it is to ensure that MPs are in the House of Commons to vote on important bills called three line whips. Defying a three-line whip is very serious, and has occasionally resulted in the whip being withdrawn from an MP. This means that the Member is effectively expelled from their party (but keeps their seat) and must sit as an Independent until the whip is restored. **(3 marks, 2 KU and 1 analysis)**

Section 2: Social Issues in the United Kingdom

Question	General marking instructions for this type of question	Max. mark	Specific marking instructions for this question
3	The candidate is required to interpret/ evaluate up to three complex sources in order to reach conclusions. In order to achieve credit candidates must show evidence which explains the conclusions reached. • Award up to 3 marks for appropriate use of evidence depending on the quality of the explanation and the synthesis of the evidence to reach any one conclusion. • For full marks candidates must refer to all sources in their answer. • For full marks candidates must reach conclusions about each of the points given and make an overall conclusion on the issue.	8	What conclusions can be drawn about gender equality in the UK? Candidates can be credited in a number of ways up to a maximum of 8 marks. **Possible approaches to answering the question:** **The effects of having children on female employment:** *Having children has a negative effect on female employment. This is supported by Source A which shows that in the last ten years the number of women forced out of their jobs – either when they become pregnant or on their return to work after giving birth – has almost doubled.* **(1 mark)** *This is supported by Source B, which shows that up to 60,000 women are sacked each year simply for being pregnant and each year an estimated 440,000 women lose out on pay or promotion as a result of pregnancy.* **(2 marks)** *This pay effect is further supported by Source A as it is estimated that for each year a mother is absent from the workplace her future wages will reduce by 5%.* **(3 marks, complex synthesis between sources A and B and conclusion)** **The existence of the gender pay gap:** *Progress towards getting rid of the gender pay gap continues to be slow. This is supported by Source B's Factfile, which shows that the full-time gender pay gap is 10%, and the average part-time pay gap is 34.5%, and approximately 70% of people in national minimum wage jobs are women.* **(1 mark)**

This is supported by the following point from Source B: 'It will be 2095 before the world's pay gap at work and equality gap in management are eliminated. That is 81 years away.' **(2 marks, detailed synthesis within a source)** In addition, according to Source C statistics the UK in 2010–2014 has an overall higher median and mean pay gap than Scotland on its own. In 2014 the UK pay gap was 14% whilst Scotland's was only 11%. **(3 marks)**

Possible overall conclusion about gender inequality in the workplace:

It is clear that gender inequalities still exist in a range of different areas involving pay, employment and other areas of life and that more has to be done to get rid of them. **(1 mark)**

Gender inequalities exist in many walks of life. Women are employed below their skills, are more likely to be employed at minimum wage and suffer real difficulties when it comes to having children. The pay gap continues to persist and the UK is being outdone by the Scandinavian countries in solving these issues. **(2 marks, valid overall conclusion supported by evidence)**

Please note that a valid conclusion that is not supported with relevant source evidence should be given no credit.

12	Analyse the success of government policies in tackling income inequality. Candidates can be credited in a number of ways up to a maximum of 12 marks. **Credit reference to aspects of the following:** • Evidence of income inequalities in Scotland/UK, e.g. statistics on poverty. • Government approaches to tackling poverty – individualist approach/ collectivist approach. • Available benefits for those on a low-income including recent changes, e.g. move to Universal Credit.
4a	An analysis mark should be awarded where a candidate uses their knowledge and understanding/a source to identify relevant components (e.g. of an idea, theory, argument, etc.) and clearly shows at least one of the following: • Links between different components. • Links between component(s) and the whole. • Links between component(s) and related concepts.

- Similarities and contradictions, consistency and inconsistency.
- Different views/interpretations.
- Possible consequences/implications.
- The relative importance of components.
- Understanding of underlying order or structure.

Credit responses that make reference to:

- Government policies to tackle income inequalities.
- An analysis of the success of policies.

Up to 8 marks for KU (description, explanation and exemplification) and up to 4 marks for analytical comments.

Award up to 6 marks per point.

Candidates may make reference to specific groups facing income inequality on the basis of, for example:

- gender
- race
- disability

- Other policies such as changes to minimum wage/living wage introduction.
- An assessment of the success of these policies, e.g. fewer people in poverty, criticisms of welfare cuts – bedroom tax/use of food banks.
- Credit also accurate references to other groups, e.g. ethnic minorities, gender inequalities, people with disabilities etc., which refer specifically to income inequalities.

Any other valid point that meets the criteria described in the general marking principles for this type of question.

Possible approaches to answering the question:

In the UK we have a welfare state that provides support for people who are in need. For those that have lost their jobs and become unemployed there is Jobseekers Allowance to support them while they look for a job and for those who do work but are on a low income, their income can be topped up by Tax Credits. **(2 marks, accurate point plus an example)**

Despite the UK being a rich country, huge inequalities exist in income. Many people live in poverty around parts of the UK and it is thought that 1 in 4 children live in poverty, although some suggest the number might be higher. **(1 mark, KU)**

Since 2010 the number has increased due to changes to benefits introduced by the Conservative government. The Conservatives have tried to tackle the problem of welfare dependency – where people feel that it pays more to live on benefits as opposed to working. One way that they have tried to do this is by introducing a benefit cap of £23,000 per family. This might be one factor that has contributed to the numbers living in poverty. **(2 marks, 1 KU example and 1 mark analysis)**

3 marks total

	12	Analyse the reasons why health inequalities continue to exist. Candidates can be credited in a number of ways up to a maximum of 12 marks. **Credit reference to aspects of the following:** • Poor lifestyle choices include smoking, excess alcohol consumption, lack of exercise, a diet high in salt and fat, drug misuse, or other risk-taking activities. • Failure to make best use of preventative care services. • Reference to government policies or health initiatives where it is acknowledged that these are a response to poor lifestyle choices, e.g. minimum alcohol pricing. • Reference to official reports, e.g. Equally Well 2008 (and Inequalities Task Force Report 2010). Which make the connection between poverty and poor health. • Statistical examples that highlight poor health in Scotland or the UK. Any other valid point that meets the criteria described in the general marking principles for this type of question.
Candidates should be credited up to full marks if they answer within a Scottish context only, a UK context only or refer to both Scotland and the UK as appropriate. Where a candidate makes more analytical points than are required to gain the maximum allocation of 4 marks, these can be credited as knowledge and understanding marks, provided they meet the criteria for this.	4b	An analysis mark should be awarded where a candidate uses their knowledge and understanding/a source to identify relevant components (e.g. of an idea, theory, argument, etc.) and clearly shows at least one of the following: • Links between different components. • Links between component(s) and the whole. • Links between component(s) and related concepts. • Similarities and contradictions. • Consistency and inconsistency. • Different views/interpretations. • Possible consequences/implications. • The relative importance of components.

Possible approaches to answering the question:

Health inequalities continue to persist around the UK. The wealthier south of England has a much higher life expectancy than poorer northern parts of the UK including Scotland. The gap can be as much as 7 years taking gender into account. **(2 marks, KU)**

Despite government action to tackle smoking, many people still smoke and this has a negative effect on their health. Smoking has been reduced by the smoking ban introduced in 2006 and this has led to a 14% decrease in heart attacks. **(2 marks, knowledge)** However, people living in deprived areas are much more likely to persist in smoking. For example, 54% of people in Glasgow Easterhouse continue to smoke compared to 16% in the more affluent suburb of Glasgow Kelvinside. People in wealthier areas are much more likely to give up smoking in response to health education whereas people in more deprived areas may feel that their lives are too stressful and lacking other enjoyment so struggle to be able to kick the habit. They are also more likely to see everyone around them smoking and so continue. **(5 marks, 3 marks knowledge and 2 analysis)**

- Understanding of underlying order or structure.

Credit responses that make reference to:

- The nature of health inequalities.

- An analysis of the reasons they continue to exist, despite measures to stop them.

Up to 8 marks for KU (description, explanation and exemplification) and up to 4 marks for analytical comments. Award up to 6 marks per point.

Candidates should be credited up to full marks if they answer within a Scottish context only, a UK context only or refer to both Scotland and the UK as appropriate.

Where a candidate makes more analytical points than are required to gain the maximum allocation of 4 marks, these can be credited as knowledge and understanding marks, provided they meet the criteria for this.

4c		12

An analysis mark should be awarded where a candidate uses their knowledge and understanding/a source to identify relevant components (e.g. of an idea, theory, argument, etc.) and clearly shows at least one of the following:

- Links between different components.
- Links between component(s) and the whole.
- Links between component(s) and related concepts.
- Similarities and contradictions.
- Consistency and inconsistency.
- Different views/interpretations/possible consequences/implications.
- The relative importance of components.
- Understanding of underlying order or structure.

Credit responses that make reference to:

- Policies to tackle crime.
- An analysis of the success of these policies in tackling crime.

Analyse the success of government policies in tackling crime.

Candidates can be credited in a number of ways up to a maximum of 12 marks.

Credit reference to aspects of the following:

The Scottish Government and UK Government have introduced or extended a range of policies to reduce crime or improve crime prevention that focus on greater punishment including:

- Policies to tackle antisocial behaviour.
- Policies on counteracting the threat of terrorism.
- Drugs – recovery and enforcement.
- Tougher sanctions on crime linked to racial, religious or social prejudice.
- Tough enforcement and prevention measures.
- Tackling serious organised crime in Scotland.
- Reforming rape and sexual offences laws.
- Tackling misuse of firearms and air weapons in Scotland.
- Youth justice measures – early intervention and tackling youth crime.
- Introducing specialist drug courts.
- Success of prisons/fines/community orders as a punishment.
- Also credit measures which focus more on rehabilitation, like restorative approaches.

Up to 8 marks for KU (description, explanation and exemplification) and up to 4 marks for analytical comments. Award up to 6 marks per point.

Candidates should be credited up to full marks if they answer within a Scottish context only, a UK context only or refer to both Scotland and the UK as appropriate. Where a candidate makes more analytical points than are required to gain the maximum allocation of 4 marks, these can be credited as knowledge and understanding marks provided they meet the criteria for this.

References can be made to Scottish and/or UK-based crime reduction policies.

Any other valid point that meets the criteria described in the general marking principles for this type of question.

Possible approaches to answering the question:

To try and reduce crime in Scotland the Scottish Government has announced it will increase the mandatory sentence for carrying a knife from four to five years. The Scottish Government hopes this will stop young people carrying knives. **(1 mark, KU, accurate and relevant point)**

The Criminal Justice and Licensing (Scotland) Act 2010 strengthened the law in terms of racial or religiously motivated crime. Now, where it has been proved that someone has committed an offence on grounds of race or religion (hate crimes), the courts must take this into account when handing out the sentence. This can lead to a longer custodial sentence or higher fine or a different type of punishment where appropriate. **(2 marks, KU)** *Although many people support tougher punishments for hate crimes, arguing this will make some people think twice before committing a crime, there are those who believe longer or tougher sentencing is the wrong approach. These people would argue that there is little evidence that tougher sentencing for hate crimes works.* **(2 marks, analysis) (4 marks, one accurate developed point, with exemplification and extended analysis)**

12		Analyse the ways in which offenders and their families are affected.
		Candidates can be credited in a number of ways up to a maximum of 12 marks.
		Credit reference to aspects of the following:
		• Reference to official crime figures.
		• Economic effects – loss of job and earning potential to themselves and their families; social effects – isolation from community.
		• Effect on children of offenders and separation from mothers/fathers.
		• Range of types of offenders, e.g. violent and non-violent.
		• Credit case studies and examples with reference to different types of offenders and crimes.
		Any other valid point that meets the criteria described in the general marking principles for this type of question.
		Possible approaches to answering the question:
		Committing a crime can have a serious effect on your ability to do your job. Those that have been found guilty of drink driving will lose their driving license for at least a year, which means they can't drive to their job or do their job anymore, which impacts on the family finances. The ability to get a job or travel to the USA in the future may be affected as you may have a criminal record for up to 20 years. **(2 marks, accurate point explained plus analysis)**
4d		An analysis mark should be awarded where a candidate uses their knowledge and understanding/a source to identify relevant components (e.g. of an idea, theory, argument, etc.) and clearly shows at least one of the following:
		• Links between different components.
		• Links between component(s) and the whole.
		• Links between component(s) and related concepts.
		• Similarities and contradictions.
		• Consistency and inconsistency.
		• Different views/interpretations.
		• Possible consequences/implications.
		• The relative importance of components.
		• Understanding of underlying order or structure.
		Credit responses that make reference to:
		• A range of different case studies of crimes.
		• An analysis of the consequences of crime for offenders and their families.

Children of offenders can be hugely affected by the imprisonment of a parent, especially if they are a from a lone-parent family. Studies conducted through the charity Barnardo's state that there is evidence to show the needs of these children are not being met. They say children who have a parent in prison can undergo a traumatic experience and often suffer in silence, unseen and unheard. It is thought that 27,000 children in Scotland suffer in this way but there is no support in place for them. Many end up going into care or relying on family support. Relationships suffer because it's not always practical to get to see their parent in prison. Studies have also shown children of offenders are up to three times more likely to develop mental health issues compared to their peers, and issues faced can include emotional and health related problems, lower results in school and declining relationships with close family. Changes to the law to support children of offenders have been called for by these charities. **(5 marks, 3 KU and 2 analysis)**

Up to 8 marks for KU (description, explanation and exemplification) and up to 4 marks for analytical comments. Award up to 6 marks per point.

Candidates should be credited up to full marks if they answer within a Scottish context only, a UK context only or refer to both Scotland and the UK as appropriate.

Where a candidate makes more analytical points than are required to gain the maximum allocation of 4 marks, these can be credited as knowledge and understanding marks provided they meet the criteria for this.

Section 3: International Issues

Question	General marking instructions for this type of question	Max. mark	Specific marking instructions for this question
5a	An analysis mark should be awarded where a candidate uses their knowledge and understanding/a source to identify relevant components (e.g. of an idea, theory, argument, etc.) and clearly shows at least one of the following: • Links between different components. • Links between component(s) and the whole. • Links between component(s) and related concepts. • Similarities and contradictions. • Consistency and inconsistency. • Different views/interpretations. • Possible consequences/implications. • The relative importance of components. • Understanding of underlying order or structure.	20	'The constitutional arrangements and institutions of a country should ensure that no branch of government has too much power.' Discuss. Candidates can be credited in a number of ways up to a maximum of 20 marks. **Credit reference to aspects of the following:** **World Power: USA** • The Constitution/amendments to it. • Three branches of Federal Government – Executive, Legislative and Judiciary. • Discussion of how each branch acts as a check on the power of the others. • System and timing of elections. • Power of state governments. Any other valid point that meets the criteria described in the general marking principles for this type of question. **Possible approaches to answering the question – USA:** *The Head of State in the USA is the President who is elected every 4 years. The powers of the President are set out in the US Constitution. The President – as the Head of the Executive – has a lot of power. The office plays a key role in National Security, the appointment of key members of the Federal Government such as*

Supreme Court Justices and in the approval of new legislation. However, these powers are subject to checks and balances by Congress and the Supreme Court. **(3 marks, 2 knowledge and 1 analysis)**

Congress plays a key role in making laws as they are the legislative arm of the Federal Government. Once a bill has been passed through both houses of Congress, however, it must be approved by the President in order for it to become a law. The President can refuse to sign a bill if he disagrees with it – this is called a veto. The bill is returned to Congress with a list of reasons as to why it was vetoed. This veto can only be returned with a two-thirds majority in both Houses of Congress to overturn it, which is quite high. Similarly, in law making the President can propose a bill but has to get a member of Congress to submit it. However, the President can bypass Congress by passing Executive Orders. Obama has passed Executive Orders on issues such as sanctions in the Middle East, climate change and HIV. Therefore, although there is a strict system of checks and balances in place, there are opportunities for the President to get his own way. **(6 marks, knowledge and conclusion with examples)**

World Power: China

- Power of the CPC.

- The role of other political parties in China.

- The main institutions of the Chinese government, e.g. Politburo, National People's Congress.

- Political participation and elections.

Any other valid point that meets the criteria described in the general marking principles for this type of question.

Evaluation involves making a judgement based on criteria, drawing conclusions on the extent to which a view is supported by the evidence; counter-arguments including possible alternative interpretations; the overall impact/ significance of the factors when taken together; the relative importance of factors in relation to the context.

Credit reference to:

- The political system used in the world power studied.

- Analysis of the ways the system checks government.

- Balanced overall evaluative comment on the effectiveness of the political system in providing a check on government.

- Provide a clear, coherent line of argument.

Up to 8 marks for KU (description, explanation and exemplification) and up to 12 marks for analytical/ evaluative comments.

Award up to 6 marks per point.

Candidates may make reference to any member of the G20 group of countries, excluding the United Kingdom.

Possible approaches to answering the question – China:

The Communist Party of China has absolute control over the Chinese government. Free elections apart from at village level are banned in China and so is the existence of any real opposition parties. **(1 mark, KU)**

China functions as a one party state in which all aspects of social, economic and political life are dominated by the Communist Party. Indeed, the Chinese Constitution includes the word 'dictatorship'. The Communist Party has absolute control over the Chinese government in the form of the Politburo, which elects through backroom negotiations the seven-person Standing Committee, which functions as the epicentre of the Communist Party's power and leadership. Xi Jinping, who took over from Hu Jintao in 2012, sits atop the system as leader of all branches of government – General Secretary; as president and head of the military, he exerts enormous influence on government policy. The premier, Li Keqiang, heads the State Council, China's equivalent of a Cabinet. This shows that one party – the Communist Party – controls the government and government policy and therefore all branches of power and has complete power. **(5 marks, 4KU and 1 analysis)**

5b	20	To what extent does a world power you have studied have influence over other world powers?

Candidates can be credited in a number of ways up to a maximum of 20 marks.

Credit reference to aspects of the following:

- Influence over other world powers in relation to conflicts.
- Influence over world powers in relation to trade and the economy.
- Influence over other world powers in relation to language and culture. |
| | | An analysis mark should be awarded where a candidate uses their knowledge and understanding/a source to identify relevant components (e.g. of an idea, theory, argument, etc.) and clearly shows at least one of the following:

- Links between different components.
- Links between component(s) and the whole. |

Possible approaches to answering the question – USA:

- Special relationship with UK.
- Relationship with G7 and G20 countries.
- Political power and influence in conflict, e.g. Syria.
- USA trading power.
- USA recession effect on the rest of the world.
- Language/culture effect.

Any other valid point that meets the criteria described in the general marking principles for this type of question.

The USA's position as a world superpower has led to it having a massive influence in media and language. Over 2 billion speak some English in the world today with the majority of them speaking an Americanised version of it. This means that the US has amazing reach with its economy, especially in the media involving TV programmes, films, videogames and music as not only does it have a large domestic market of more than 300 million customers it can also reach out and sell to the rest of the world and has done so successfully. **(2 marks, knowledge and evaluative comments)**

The USA is one of the 5 permanent members of the Security Council along with the UK, China, Russia and France. It can have a large influence on what actions the UN can take in stopping conflict around the world. Conflict in Syria has been a major issue as there has been a civil war between President Assad and his opponents. A resolution has been agreed to investigate and rid Syria of chemical weapons which have been used on innocent people. This resolution is thanks largely to the diplomatic efforts of the US – originally, Russia had opposed and vetoed any UN action. **(3 marks, knowledge and analysis)**

- Links between component(s) and related concepts.
- Similarities and contradictions.
- Consistency and inconsistency.
- Different views/interpretations.
- Possible consequences/implications.
- The relative importance of components.
- Understanding of underlying order or structure.

Evaluation involves making a judgement based on criteria, drawing conclusions on the extent to which a view is supported by the evidence; counter-arguments including possible alternative interpretations; the overall impact/ significance of the factors when taken together; the relative importance of factors in relation to the context.

Credit responses that make reference to:

- Role/part played by the world power.
- Balanced overall evaluative comment on the extent to which said world power has an influence on other countries.

• Provide a clear, coherent line of argument. Up to 8 marks for KU (description, explanation and exemplification) and up to 12 marks for analytical/evaluative comments. Award up to 6 marks per point. Candidates may make reference to any member of the G20 group of countries, excluding the United Kingdom.	**Possible approaches to answering the question – China:** • Influence as a superpower on the economy • Trading power • Role in UN Security Council Any other valid point that meets the criteria described in the general marking principles for this type of question. *Despite being an emerging market, China is the world's second largest economy and has tremendous influence on the global economy and financial markets. In the last decade it has contributed more than 30% to global economic growth, according to some statistics. After experiencing large growth for decades China's economy is beginning to slow – it is estimated that after 2020 economic growth will slow to 4% annually. China's growth had been led by its urbanisation, its property boom and demand from its growing middle class. As the economy has slowed and demand has reduced, this has had an impact internationally. The economies of countries that export commodities to China are feeling the impact. Australia's economy for example, relies heavily on exports to China.* **(5 marks, 2 KU and 3 analysis and evaluation)**

5c	20	Discuss whether international organisations have made significant progress in resolving a world issue you have studied.

Discuss whether international organisations have made significant progress in resolving a world issue you have studied.

Candidates can be credited in a number of ways up to a maximum of 20 marks.

Credit reference to aspects of the following:

- Work of the main international organisations – UN, NATO, EU as well as NGOs.
- Actions taken to resolve a world issue.
- Success of these actions.

Any other valid point that meets the criteria described in the general marking principles for this type of question.

Possible approaches to answering the question:

World Issue – Lack of development in Africa:

The UN plays a significant role in attempting to deal with development issues in Africa and does this through its specialised agencies. UNICEF deals with helping children in need along with their mothers. It has run a campaign called Schools for Africa across 13 countries in Sub-Saharan and West Africa, where two out of five children do not have access to primary school – due to poverty, illness, disability, armed conflict, natural disaster, gender inequity or simply because they live in remote rural areas. As many as half of all primary school pupils drop out of school. Twelve million pupils across the continent have been helped to a better school experience so it could be argued that significant progress has been made. However poverty continues in Africa despite the achievements of the UN agencies. **(4 marks, KU including exemplification and analysis)**

An analysis mark should be awarded where a candidate uses their knowledge and understanding/a source to identify relevant components (e.g. of an idea, theory, argument, etc.) and clearly shows at least one of the following:

- Links between different components.
- Links between component(s) and the whole.
- Links between component(s) and related concepts.
- Similarities and contradictions.
- Consistency and inconsistency.
- Different views/interpretations.
- Possible consequences/implications.
- The relative importance of components.
- Understanding of underlying order or structure.

Evaluation involves making a judgement based on criteria, drawing conclusions on the extent to which a view is supported by the evidence; counter-arguments including possible alternative interpretations; the overall impact/significance of the factors when taken together; the relative importance of factors in relation to the context.

World Issue – Terrorism:

Terrorism poses a real and serious threat to the security and safety of the world population. It is a global threat that knows no border, nationality or religion – a challenge that the international community must tackle together. NATO is an organisation of 28 countries including the USA, Canada, UK and many European countries. It has many strategies in place including cyber-terrorism strategies, securing major events and working out strategies in case of an attack. It also works in Afghanistan to get rid of the Taliban and establish a proper democracy. It has helped to train the police force to ensure that peace continues. Despite these attempts, ISIL continues to be a major threat in the Middle East, with Turkey continuing to be subject to attacks. **(5 marks, 4 knowledge and 1 analysis)**

Credit reference to:

- Attempts to solve a world issue.
- The success of these attempts by international organisations.
- Provide a clear, coherent line of argument.

Up to 8 marks for KU (description, explanation and exemplification) and up to 12 marks for analytical/evaluative comments. Award up to 6 marks per point.

Candidates may make reference to any world issue the impact of which extends beyond the boundaries of any single country.

20	To what extent has a world issue you have studied had an impact on the international community? Candidates can be credited in a number of ways up to a maximum of 20 marks. **Credit reference to aspects of the following:** - Terrorism - Migration/immigration - Effects of conflicts – refugees - Economic difficulties, e.g. European countries such as Greece Any other valid point that meets the criteria described in the general marking principles for this type of question.
5d	An analysis mark should be awarded where a candidate uses their knowledge and understanding/a source to identify relevant components (e.g. of an idea, theory, argument, etc.) and clearly shows at least one of the following: - Links between different components. - Links between component(s) and the whole. - Links between component(s) and related concepts.

Possible approaches to answering the question:

Terrorism has no boundaries and is a major issue for the world community. Many countries in the world have experienced the horror of an attack that has led to the death of its people, as well as terror and destruction. The UK has experienced it through the Glasgow Airport attacks and London 7/7 when more than 50 people were killed from explosions on buses and tube lines after an Al-Qaeda attack. More recently, terrorist attacks have come from ISIL where Westerners in Iraq and Syria have been the victims of beheadings and other brutality. Obviously, these terrorist attacks have had a major impact internationally. **(3 marks, 2 KU and 1 evaluative comment)**

Conflict and war have had a major impact on the international community. The civil war between President Assad's forces and his opponents has had a huge effect on those caught up in the conflict. As a result of the horrors of war such as murder, rape and abduction and the side effects – lack of access to food, water, medical care and education, many innocent Syrians have decided to leave and look for a better life elsewhere. Almost 4 million people have fled Syria since the start of the conflict, most of them women and children. It is one of the largest refugee exoduses in recent history. Neighbouring countries have borne the brunt of the refugee crisis, with Lebanon, Jordan and Turkey struggling to accommodate the flood of new arrivals. In September 2015, the refugee crisis started to have a dramatic impact on Europe as many refugees crossed over to Greece and Turkey by boat and made their way to the Western European countries such as Germany and Austria where at first they were welcomed. Many countries like Hungary have ended up closing their borders because they couldn't keep up with the demand. There are calls for more 'burden sharing' across all the EU countries as countries like Germany struggle to cope with the number of refugees. This is one way in which the conflict in Syria has had a major impact on the international community. **(6 marks, 4 knowledge and 2 analysis with evaluative comment)**

- Similarities and contradictions.
- Consistency and inconsistency.
- Different views/interpretations.
- Possible consequences/implications.
- The relative importance of components.
- Understanding of underlying order or structure.

Evaluation involves making a judgement based on criteria, drawing conclusions on the extent to which a view is supported by the evidence; counter-arguments including possible alternative interpretations; the overall impact/significance of the factors when taken together; the relative importance of factors in relation to the context.

Credit responses that make reference to:

- An explanation of the international issue.
- Balanced overall evaluative comment on how much the international community is affected by the issue.
- Provide a clear, coherent line of argument.

Up to 8 marks for KU (description, explanation and exemplification) and up to 12 marks for analytical/evaluative comments. Award up to 6 marks per point.

The impact may be regional or global in scale.

Candidates may make reference to any world issue the impact of which extends beyond the boundaries of any single country.

Mark Scheme for Exam B

Section 1: Democracy in Scotland and the United Kingdom

Question	General marking instructions for this type of question	Max. mark	Specific marking instructions for this question
1a	An analysis mark should be awarded where a candidate uses their knowledge and understanding/a source to identify relevant components (e.g. of an idea, theory, argument, etc.) and clearly shows at least one of the following: • Links between different components. • Links between component(s) and the whole. • Links between component(s) and related concepts. • Similarities and contradictions. • Consistency and inconsistency. • Different views/interpretations. • Possible consequences/implications. • The relative importance of components. • Understanding of underlying order or structure.	20	Discuss the different factors that are more likely to affect voting behaviour. Candidates can be credited in a number of ways up to a maximum of 20 marks. **Credit reference to aspects of the following:** • Long-term factors like social class, age, race, religion, location, family background. • Short-term factors like different forms of media, party leadership, context of the election. • Credit also answers that deal with issues affecting turnout such as the context of the election for example. Any other valid point that meets the criteria described in the general marking principles for this type of question. **Possible approaches to answering the question:** *Social class is less of a factor in determining voter behaviour in recent elections than it was in the post-war years. However, more AB voters vote Conservative and more DE voters vote Labour, showing that it is still an influence.* **(1 mark, analysis)** *Party leadership has become more of an important factor in recent years. In the 2011 Scottish Parliament elections, Labour had a lead in the opinion polls and were on course to win. However, it is thought that the Labour leader Iain Grey wasn't seen to be a future leader and lacked charisma.* **(2 marks, KU with exemplification and limited analysis)**

This was demonstrated by the Subway-gate incident that took place – Iain Grey was seen as 'running away' from some protestors and went to hide in a branch of Subway. His popularity and that of Scottish Labour took a dip after that and the SNP went on to win the election with a majority. **(1 mark, analysis)** *Party leadership could therefore be seen as a major factor as Alex Salmond was very much seen as leadership material at the time. However, it could also be linked to the fact that the SNP popularity was rising anyway.* **(1 mark, evaluative comment) (4 marks, knowledge with analysis, exemplification and evaluative statement)**

Evaluation involves making a judgement based on criteria, drawing conclusions on the extent to which a view is supported by the evidence; counter-arguments including possible alternative interpretations; the overall impact/ significance of the factors when taken together; the relative importance of factors in relation to the context.

Credit responses that make reference to:

- Long and short-term factors which may influence the way people vote and/or turn out to vote.

- An analysis of how much of an impact they are likely to make.

- Balanced overall evaluative comment on the extent of the various factors on influencing voting.

- Provide a clear, coherent line of argument.

Up to 8 marks for KU (description, explanation and exemplification) and up to 12 marks for analytical/ evaluative comments. Award up to 6 marks per point.

1b	20	To what extent can people participate in and influence the political system?

Candidates can be credited in a number of ways up to a maximum of 20 marks.

Credit reference to aspects of the following:

- Voting in elections – general, Scottish, local, European – with aim of influencing who runs the country.

- Joining political parties with the aim of influencing policy and voting for party leaders.

- Joining a pressure group with aim of influencing government policy.

Any other valid point that meets the criteria described in the general marking principles for this type of question.

Possible approaches to answering the question:

UK citizens can join a pressure group with the aim of changing government policy in a certain area, e.g. Greenpeace aims to influence government policy on the environment. **(1 mark, KU)**

UK citizens can join a pressure group with the aim of changing government policy in a certain area through a variety of methods, e.g. Greenpeace have campaigned against the dangers of fracking by demonstrating in large numbers near to where the fracking was taking place. This made the news headlines as an MP, Caroline Lucas, got arrested. This led to more people becoming aware of fracking and its pros and cons and may have influenced their vote. **(3 marks, knowledge with analysis and exemplification)**

An analysis mark should be awarded where a candidate uses their knowledge and understanding/a source to identify relevant components (e.g. of an idea, theory, argument, etc.) and clearly shows at least one of the following:

- Links between different components.

- Links between component(s) and the whole.

- Links between component(s) and related concepts.

- Similarities and contradictions.

- Consistency and inconsistency.

- Different views/interpretations.

- Possible consequences/implications.

- The relative importance of components.

- Understanding of underlying order or structure.

Pressure groups can be insider or outsider. Insider groups have a much better chance of changing government policy as they work with the government and provide them with key information, e.g. Age Concern have shaped government policy on housing and welfare benefits for the elderly. **(2 marks, analysis and exemplification)**

5 marks total

UK citizens have a number of different opportunities to vote for representatives who will speak on their behalf in parliament. The people who are voted for will determine which political parties lead our governments and local councils. **(1 mark, KU)** *In 2015, people voted in the general election to elect MPs and determine which party would form the UK government. Many people argue that the First Past the Post electoral system is unfair as a lot of votes are wasted – many votes do not contribute to the winning candidate who becomes MP. This was demonstrated by the SNP – they won 56 MPs with 4% of the vote, however UKIP gained 12% of the vote and only 1 MP. In certain areas, many people's vote does not count and therefore has no impact on who forms the government.* **(3 marks, KU, analysis and exemplification)**

4 marks total

Evaluation involves making a judgement based on criteria, drawing conclusions on the extent to which a view is supported by the evidence; counter-arguments including possible alternative interpretations; the overall impact/ significance of the factors when taken together; the relative importance of factors in relation to the context.

Credit responses that refer to:

- Different ways in which people can participate in the political system.

- Analysis of the different ways people can participate in politics.

- Balanced overall evaluative comment on whether people are having an influence in politics.

- Provide a clear, coherent line of argument.

Up to 8 marks for KU (description, explanation and exemplification) and up to 12 marks for analytical/ evaluative comments. Award up to 6 marks per point.

Section 2: Social Issues in the UK

Question	General marking instructions for this type of question	Max. mark	Specific marking instructions for this question
2	The candidate is required to interpret/evaluate up to three complex sources of information, detecting and explaining the extent of objectivity. In order to achieve credit candidates must show evidence that supports the extent of accuracy in a given viewpoint. • Award up to 3 marks for appropriate use of evidence depending on the quality of the explanation and the synthesis of the evidence for any one explanation of the extent of objectivity. • For full marks candidates must refer to all sources in their answer. • For full marks candidates must make an overall judgement as to the extent of the accuracy of the given statement. • Maximum of 6 marks if no overall judgement made on extent of accuracy of the statement. Candidates may be awarded up to a maximum of 2 marks for incorporating an evaluation of the reliability of the sources in their explanations, although this is not mandatory.	8	'Taking children out of school in term time is wrong and damages their education.' Candidates can be credited in a number of ways up to a maximum of 8 marks. **Evidence that supports the view:** • Source A – pupils must get a full-time education (DoE guidance). • Source A – pupils can only get out of this under exceptional circumstances and permission from head teacher. • Source A – consequences of taking children out of school are fines and possible prosecution. • Source B – schools operate properly if children attend all through term-time. • Source B – sends out the wrong message about education. • Source B – disruption in learning that needs to be caught up. **Possible responses:** *In Source A the Department of Education states that every child should get a full time education and can only be allowed away from school under exceptional circumstances as agreed by the head teacher.* **(1 mark, relevant information)**

In Source A the Department of Education states that every child should get a full-time education and can only be allowed away from school under exceptional circumstances as agreed by the head teacher. This is underlined by the fact that those who take their child out of school under non-exceptional circumstances face a fine and those who refuse to pay could end up with a more severe punishment, including prison. This backs up the view that taking children out of school is wrong. **(2 marks, 2 relevant pieces of information from within the same source)**

In Source A the Department of Education states that every child should get a full-time education and can only be allowed away from school under exceptional circumstances as agreed by the head teacher. This is underlined by the fact that those who take their child out of school under non-exceptional circumstances face a fine and those who refuse to pay could end up with a more severe punishment, including prison. Source B supports this by saying: '…We do want to make sure that children come to school. They don't have their education disrupted or the education of others in the classroom when they come back and try to get them up to speed with other children.' This evidence supports the view that taking children out of school disrupts their education. **(3 marks, synthesis between sources)**

Evidence that does not support the view:

- Source B – no harm in taking children out of school a week early at the end of summer term when they might not miss anything (e.g. watching DVDs).

- Source B – education doesn't always happen in the classroom (e.g. rock climbing).

- Source C – a majority of people would risk a fine to enjoy holidays in term-time.

- Source C – increase in number of people getting fines in Hull and North East Lincolnshire.

- Source C – nearly a quarter of a million signatures on the petition to remove term-time fines.

Possible responses:

Source B says... family holidays create amazing memories and experiences. Education isn't just about being in the classroom ...rock climbing experiences. Source C backs this by showing that a significant number of families would risk a fine to take their children out of school – two-thirds of families asked said they would risk a fine and take their children out of school, a further 11% said no but they had done it in the past. Source C further shows that the number of families receiving fines has increased in Hull and North East Lincolnshire which shows more parents don't believe they are harming their child's education. **(3 marks, relevant information and evaluative comment)**

Candidates may also be credited up to 2 marks on any comment/ evaluation of the origin and reliability of the sources:

The Department of Education website reflects the policy of the UK government so could be regarded as being very reliable and factual. The survey conducted by the Telegraph only asked 380 people so could be regarded as unreliable – a bigger sample may produce different results. The 38 Degrees website is obviously clearly biased against the government's position so this has to be taken into account. **(2 marks)**

For full marks, candidates must make an overall judgement as to the extent of the accuracy of the given statement:

Overall, the evidence does support the view as there is clear support from a number of different sources about the unpopularity of fining parents. The 38 degrees website shows an increasing number of people who think the policy is wrong and the government should change their policy. **(2 marks)**

Question	Expected Answer	Max Mark
3a	Evaluate the different theories that best explain one inequality of your choice. Candidates can be credited in a number of ways up to a maximum of 12 marks. **Credit reference to aspects of the following:** - Income and wealth inequalities – reference to unemployment, low pay, social exclusion, education. - Gender inequalities – low pay, gender stereotyping, part-time working due to family commitments, glass ceiling, lone-parenthood. - Race inequalities – (need to address different ethnic minorities), culture, education, discrimination. - Health inequalities – age, race and gender, social class, poverty, lifestyle choices. Any other valid point that meets the criteria described in the general marking principles for this type of question. **Possible approaches to answering the question:** *Many families who live in poverty actually have at least one member in work. These 'working poor' may be on a zero-hour contract or earning minimum wage.* **(1 mark, KU)** *Lone-parent families are more likely to be headed by a woman. Employment opportunities are likely to be limited, as someone has to be there for the children finishing school or else pay for expensive private childcare. Family income therefore is more likely to be limited to surviving on benefits such as tax credits or doing part-time work, which is more likely to be low paid. Family structure, i.e. how many parents are in a family, is therefore a very significant reason as to why income inequalities exist.* **(3 marks, KU with evaluative comments)**	12

Evaluation involves making a judgement(s) based on criteria, drawing conclusions on the extent to which a view is supported by the evidence; counter-arguments including possible alternative interpretations; the overall impact/significance of the factors when taken together; the relative importance of factors in relation to the context.

Credit responses that make reference to:

- An explanation of different theories to explain why a certain inequality occurs.
- Evaluation of the possible theories as to whether they are a major cause of inequality.

Up to 8 marks for KU (description, explanation and exemplification) and up to 4 marks for evaluative comments.

Award up to 6 marks per point.

Candidates should be credited up to full marks if they answer within a Scottish context only, a UK context only or refer to both Scotland and the UK.

Where a candidate makes more evaluative points than are required to gain the maximum allocation of 4 marks, these can be credited as knowledge and understanding marks provided they meet the criteria for this...

		Gender inequalities continue to exist in the workplace. *Despite the fact that girls are outperforming boys at school and at university and in the early part of careers, women's careers slow down compared to men's when children come along. 17% of women believe that raising or caring for children has presented barriers to career development.* **(2 marks, KU)** *Mothers may not want to work long hours in the office and feel there is a culture of presenteeism in big corporations where a physical presence is expected for long hours. 73% of female managers believe there are barriers preventing them from progressing to the top level in the form of the glass ceiling.* **(2 marks, KU)** *As a result, there is pressure for more flexible working – at home, or flexible hours in the office, which could make a difference to women staying in the top professions. Progress has been made with gender inequality – there are many examples of progress such as more women in politics and in business, but cultural and discriminatory attitudes still have to change.* **(6 marks total, KU with analysis and evaluative comments)**
3b	12	Evaluate the success of government policies to reduce inequality. Candidates can be credited in a number of ways up to a maximum of 12 marks. **Credit reference to aspects of the following:** • Explanation of the term individualism – focusing on the individual helping themselves. • Explanation of the term collectivism – focusing on the government having a major responsibility to help those in need. • Focus on the support provided through benefits. • Changes in the tax allowance. • Welfare reform since 2010 by the Conservative party (reserved matter) and the introduction of Universal Credit. • Refer to benefit cap, bedroom tax and effects of this. Evaluation involves making a judgement(s) based on criteria, drawing conclusions on the extent to which a view is supported by the evidence; counter-arguments including possible alternative interpretations; the overall impact/ significance of the factors when taken together; the relative importance of factors in relation to the context. **Credit responses that make reference to:** • An explanation of different individualist strategies to tackle inequality. • Evaluation of the success of these strategies.

- Scottish government change of approach – more collectivist.
- Labour party under Jeremy Corbyn – more collectivist, e.g. promise to build more council houses.
- Health inequalities – evaluation of smoking ban etc.

Any other valid point that meets the criteria described in the general marking principles for this type of question.

Possible approaches to answering the question:

The government provides a wide range of benefits to help those in need, who have no other source of income or are on a low income. These benefits include Child Benefit, old age Pensions, Working Tax Credits and Universal Credit. In 2015 there was a cap introduced on the total amount of benefits a family could claim in a year. **(2 marks, KU, description of role of benefits and examples)**

One benefit paid by government to help tackle inequality is Child Benefit. This is a benefit paid to help with the additional costs of bringing up children. The amount paid is £20.70 per week for the eldest child and £13.70 for each additional child. This helps to tackle inequality as these payments are very important to those who have a very low income and make a big difference to the family income in a poor household. Child Benefit is not paid in full to households with a high income — after £50,000 the amount of child benefit paid is reduced. This means that it helps to reduce inequality as families on low income get more in benefit than high-income families. **(4 marks, 2 KU explanation of child benefit, 2 evaluation of effectiveness)**

12	

Up to 8 marks for KU (description, explanation and exemplification) and up to 4 marks for evaluative comments. Award up to 6 marks per point.

Candidates should be credited up to full marks if they answer within a Scottish context only, a UK context only or refer to both Scotland and the UK.

Where a candidate makes more evaluative points than are required to gain the maximum allocation of 4 marks these can be credited as knowledge and understanding marks provided they meet the criteria for this.

Some would claim that the benefit system is not effective in tackling inequality as the amount of benefits paid is low and well below the level of average earnings. It is also claimed that benefits can lead to people being trapped in poverty as they become dependent on benefits and have no incentive to find a job as they will lose benefits and have to pay tax, so they could be worse off in work. Universal Credit was supposed to tackle this as benefits are not totally stopped when a person finds a job and are withdrawn gradually. However, with the introduction of the benefit cap some people have found themselves in extreme poverty. **(3 marks, 1 KU and 2 evaluation of effectiveness of benefits as a way of tackling inequality)**

12	Evaluate the different theories that best explain the causes of crime.

Candidates can be credited in a number of ways up to a maximum of 12 marks.

Credit reference to aspects of the following:

- Individualist theories – those theories that focus on greed and individual choice.
- Collectivism – those linking to poverty and social deprivation.

Any other valid point that meets the criteria described in the general marking principles for this type of question.

Possible approaches to answering the question:

Collectivist theories put the emphasis on people reacting to their social circumstances and reacting against living in poverty. For example, many people who took part in the London Riots in 2011 came from poorer backgrounds and had little educational attainment. **(2 marks, knowledge with exemplification)**

Many theories such as realist theories put the blame on the individual. They blame the rise in 'fatherless families' and a decline in civility as major reasons why people commit crime. Those people who have the opportunity and see a way to benefit from crime will do it. **(2 marks, knowledge and analysis)** |
| 3c | Evaluation involves making a judgement(s) based on criteria, drawing conclusions on the extent to which a view is supported by the evidence; counter-arguments including possible alternative interpretations; the overall impact/significance of the factors when taken together; the relative importance of factors in relation to the context.

Credit responses that make reference to:

- Explaining the possible theories to explain crime.
- An evaluation of these theories.

Up to 8 marks for KU (description, explanation and exemplification) and up to 4 marks for evaluative comments.

Award up to 6 marks per point. |

	A lack of success in education causes an increase in crime. A lack of education reduces opportunities to earn high wages and, therefore, those on low wages or without any wages may be more likely to engage in criminal activity. Those with little success in education may feel let down by society and are therefore less likely to accept the rules and laws of that society. Further, less well-educated people tend to mix more with other people who are involved in criminal activity. However, some young people may learn to be more patient through schooling and place more weight on their potential future earnings rather than becoming involved in crime, e.g. stealing. **(3 marks, 1 KU and 2 analysis)**	Candidates should be credited up to full marks if they answer within a Scottish context only, a UK context only or refer to both Scotland and the UK. Where a candidate makes more evaluative points than are required to gain the maximum allocation of 4 marks these can be credited as knowledge and understanding marks, provided they meet the criteria for this.

3 marks total

| 12 | Evaluate the success of different approaches to solve crime. Candidates can be credited in a number of ways up to a maximum of 12 marks. **Credit reference to aspects of the following:** • Rehabilitation in prison • Community rehabilitation in the form of community service and/or electronic tagging • Drug rehabilitation schemes. Any other valid point that meets the criteria described in the general marking principles for this type of question. **Possible approaches to answering the question:** *One of the aims of prison is to rehabilitate offenders who are sent there. Prisons offer a variety of schemes whereby prisoners can improve their skills in education or by learning a skill.* **(1 mark, KU)** *However, this is less likely to happen when prisons are overcrowded and find it difficult to cater to all. In addition, prisoners who get short sentences cannot access these schemes – this is why the Scottish Government have moved away from short sentences of less than 3 months to more community-based schemes.* **(2 marks, analysis)** | 3d Evaluation involves making a judgement(s) based on criteria, drawing conclusions on the extent to which a view is supported by the evidence; counter-arguments including possible alternative interpretations; the overall impact/significance of the factors when taken together; the relative importance of factors in relation to the context. **Credit responses that make reference to:** • Explanation of rehabilitation schemes to tackle crime. • An evaluation of the success of these schemes. Up to 8 marks for KU (description, explanation and exemplification) and up to 4 marks for evaluative comments. |

Award up to 6 marks per point.

Candidates should be credited up to full marks if they answer within a Scottish context only, a UK context only or refer to both Scotland and the UK.

Where a candidate makes more evaluative points than are required to gain the maximum allocation of 4 marks these can be credited as knowledge and understanding marks provided they meet the criteria for this.

The Community Payback Order came into force in Scotland on 1 February 2011. Other community-based court orders include the Drug Treatment and Testing Order and the Restriction of Liberty Order (electronic tagging). The order might include a requirement to carry out hours of unpaid work in the community with benefits for the community along with completion of intensive supervision, alcohol, drug or behavioural programmes. Clearing pathways of snow and ice, building eco-plant areas for school children, repainting community centres or churches, cleaning up beaches, growing vegetables and distributing the produce to care homes and local charities, are just a few of the unpaid work activities being carried out by offenders in communities across Scotland. **(3 marks, KU)** Working in the community is thought to be better rehabilitation as offenders are working and gaining skills. They are also doing something productive and may feel a sense of worth. They are also able to keep in touch with their family and support network. However, some people worry that community sentencing is an easy option as a punishment. Repeat offending is lower for those that have been given community sentences. **(2 marks, evaluation)**

5 marks total

Section 3: International Issues

Question	General marking instructions for this type of question	Max. mark	Specific marking instructions for this question
4	The candidate is required to interpret/ evaluate up to three complex sources in order to reach conclusions. In order to achieve credit candidates must show evidence that explains the conclusions reached. • Award up to 3 marks for appropriate use of evidence depending on the quality of the explanation and the synthesis of the evidence to reach any one conclusion. • For full marks candidates must refer to all sources in their answer. • For full marks candidates must reach conclusions about each of the points given and make an overall conclusion on the issue.	8	What conclusions can be drawn about immigration in the EU? Candidates can be credited in a number of ways up to a maximum of 8 marks. **Possible approaches to answering the question:** **The level of immigration:** *The level of immigration is too high and there hasn't been any slowdown in the last 10 years. The most recent figures show immigration is at 330,000 in the year to March 2015, the highest on record as shown in Source A.* **(1 mark)** *As shown elsewhere in Source A the corresponding figure under Labour in the year to March 2005 was 320,000 – only 10,000 less. Other parts of Europe also have problems with immigration such as Greece and Germany. From Source B, ONS statistics back this up – immigration continues to increase and emigration is static.* **(3 marks, synthesis of evidence between and within Source A and Source B, with conclusion)** **Public attitudes to immigration in the UK:** *People are very concerned about immigration in the UK. In a recent opinion poll, 50% saw immigration as a major concern, as shown in Source C.* **(1 mark)** *Also from Source C we see that this is an increase of 8% on the previous year and is higher than people's concerns about the economy. From Source A it is shown that mass immigration is seen as something British people didn't want or ask for, and they are deeply concerned about the numbers of immigrants – schools are becoming overcrowded and there is a shortage of affordable housing.* **(3 marks, synthesis of information between Source A and C with conclusion)** **Possible overall conclusion on immigration:** *Immigration is a serious issue which people are very concerned about, especially as net migration is at its highest level for a decade as shown in Source B.* **(1 mark)**

Immigration is at its highest level for a decade and this picture is repeated across other European countries such as Greece and Germany as shown in Source A. People have real concerns about immigration and have identified it as one of their biggest concerns, bigger than even the economy, as shown in Source C – one reason being the major effect it has on schools and housing. **(2 marks, valid conclusion based on evidence)**

Please note that a valid conclusion that is not supported with relevant source evidence should be given no credit.

5a	12	Analyse the impact of a socio-economic issue on the citizens of the world power you have studied. Candidates can be credited in a number of ways up to a maximum of 12 marks. **Credit reference to aspects of the following:** **Relevant points: ethnic minorities in the USA** • Impact of income inequalities. • Impact of education inequalities. • Impact of health inequalities. • Inequalities in the legal system and their impact. • Any other relevant impact of a socio-economic issue. Any other valid point that meets the criteria described in the general marking principles for this type of question. **Possible approaches to answering the question:** *The USA is a very rich country. However some Black communities, especially in the inner city, can suffer extreme poverty – three times more than the White community.* **(1 mark, some exemplification)**
		An analysis mark should be awarded where a candidate uses their knowledge and understanding/a source to identify relevant components (e.g. of an idea, theory, argument, etc.) and clearly shows at least one of the following: • Links between different components. • Links between component(s) and the whole. • Links between component(s) and related concepts. • Similarities and contradictions. • Consistency and inconsistency. • Different views/interpretations. • Possible consequences/implications. • The relative importance of components.

- Understanding of underlying order or structure.

Credit responses that make reference to:

- Identify social and economic inequalities in a world power.
- An analysis of the reasons and effects of this inequality.

Up to 8 marks for KU (description, explanation and exemplification) and up to 4 marks for analytical comments. Award up to 6 marks per point.

Where a candidate makes more analytical points than are required to gain the maximum allocation of 4 marks, these can be credited as knowledge and understanding marks provided they meet the criteria for this.

One area where there is major inequality is healthcare. Healthcare in the USA is not free and those more likely to live in poverty like certain parts of the Black community are less likely to be able to afford to buy health insurance and are less likely to have a job which comes with healthcare as a perk. **(1 mark, KU)** Without health insurance, US citizens are less likely to have check-ups for minor ailments and will have to rely on overcrowded emergency rooms if seriously ill. This has resulted in lower life expectancy amongst these groups. **(1 mark, analysis)** Coupled with a higher risk lifestyle that is more likely to involve drugs and obesity, health has become a serious problem in certain communities. **(1 mark, evaluation)** Many people have taken up healthcare as a result of Obama's Affordable Care Act which makes it compulsory to buy healthcare and receive it free if they can't afford it – this was brought into force in 2014 and as a result 8 million people have healthcare in the US who didn't have it before. **(2 marks, KU) (5 marks, detailed knowledge with exemplification, analysis and evaluation)**

Relevant points: China

- Impact of rural inequalities – income, education, healthcare.
- Impact of gender inequalities.

Any other valid point that meets the criteria described in the general marking principles for this type of question.

Possible approaches to answering the question:

Around half of Chinese people live in the countryside. For most, life has improved with economic reform. Most rural Chinese have better diets, clothing and housing. More have access to electricity and the numbers of people with televisions, fridges and other consumer goods has increased. However, in 2012 an estimated 99 million rural Chinese continued to live below the poverty line having an income of less than $1 a day. **(2 marks, KU)** The CPC leadership are acutely aware that if too many Chinese people are excluded from the general increase in wealth in society this could result in serious social discontent.

As a result the Chinese government has increased investment in infrastructure, e.g. roads, electricity production, water distribution etc. in rural areas to provide jobs. Many of these projects have opened up the interior of China to foreign investment. This has resulted in increased economic growth. **(2 marks, analysis and KU)**

(4 marks)

The government has made it easier for farmers to access credit so they can invest and increase their farm incomes. Farmers have also seen their taxes cut. Increased managerial, agricultural and technical support is offered to farmers to make farm businesses more viable. The Chinese government hope this will bring about prosperity for those living in rural areas, like it has for people living in China's cities. **(3 marks, 2 KU, 1 analysis)**

12

Analyse the ways citizens can have their views represented within the political system in the world power you have studied.

Candidates can be credited in a number of ways up to a maximum of 12 marks.

Credit reference to aspects of the following:

USA

- Inequality in voting amongst ethnic minorities.
- Voting turnout very low anyway but lower amongst Blacks and Hispanics than Whites apart from Obama election.
- Joining political parties and standing as a candidate more likely for Whites and men.
- Reasons why and analysis of any attempts to solve the issue.

Any other valid point that meets the criteria described in the general marking principles for this type of question.

5b

An analysis mark should be awarded where a candidate uses their knowledge and understanding/a source to identify relevant components (e.g. of an idea, theory, argument, etc.) and clearly shows at least one of the following:

- Links between different components.
- Links between component(s) and the whole.
- Links between component(s) and related concepts.
- Similarities and contradictions.
- Consistency and inconsistency.
- Different views/interpretations.
- Possible consequences/implications.

- The relative importance of components.
- Understanding of underlying order or structure.

Credit responses that make reference to:

- Inequality in political participation.
- Analysis of the issues surrounding these inequalities.

Up to 8 marks for KU (description, explanation and exemplification) and up to 4 marks for analytical comments.

Award up to 6 marks per point.

Where a candidate makes more analytical points than are required to gain the maximum allocation of 4 marks, these can be credited as knowledge and understanding marks provided they meet the criteria for this.

Possible approaches to answering the question:

There is a proven link between level of education and turnout to vote – Blacks are more likely to have a lower level of education and therefore are less likely to vote. **(1 mark, KU)** *Turnout has traditionally been around 6% less than White turnout in Presidential elections. However, turnout increased in 2008 and 2012 with the election of Barack Obama, the first Black President. In 2012, Black turnout increased to 66%, while White turnout was 64%.* **(3 marks, 2 KU with exemplification, 1 analysis)**

China

- Political participation lower in rural areas.
- No real opposition to Communist party
- Political parties are allowed but offer no real opposition to the Communist party.
- Middle class more likely to be allowed to protest.

Any other valid point that meets the criteria described in the general marking principles for this type of question.

Possible approaches to answering the question:

China is a one-party state with the Communist party being the only party allowed to hold power. There are 8 legal political parties, apart from the CPC, including the China Democratic League but they are no real opposition to the Communist party despite being allowed to take part in government discussions. In recent years, as China has become richer, the middle class has been allowed to express opinions as to how the economy is doing. **(2 marks, KU)**

5c	12	An analysis mark should be awarded where a candidate uses their knowledge and understanding/a source to identify relevant components (e.g. of an idea, theory, argument, etc.) and clearly shows at least one of the following: • Links between different components. • Links between component(s) and the whole. • Links between component(s) and related concepts. • Similarities and contradictions. • Consistency and inconsistency. • Different views/interpretations. • Possible consequences/implications. • The relative importance of components. • Understanding of underlying order or structure.	Analyse the main causes of a world issue you have studied. Candidates can be credited in a number of ways up to a maximum of 12 marks. **Credit reference to aspects of the following:** **Relevant world issues could be:** • Lack of development • Conflict • Terrorism • Poverty • Immigration **Depending on the world issue chosen, candidates may make reference to any relevant factors, such as:** • Political factors – government structure. • Economic factors – debt, trading position. • Social factors – lack of education and health, cultural differences, inequalities. Any other valid point that meets the criteria described in the general marking principles for this type of question.

Credit responses that make reference to:

- Social, economic and political issues that cause the chosen world issue.
- Analysis of the issues surrounding these factors and the cause of the world issue.

Up to 8 marks for KU (description, explanation and exemplification) and up to 4 marks for analytical comments. Award up to 6 marks per point.

Where a candidate makes more analytical points than are required to gain the maximum allocation of 4 marks, these can be credited as knowledge and understanding marks, provided they meet the criteria for this.

Candidates may make reference to any world issue the impact of which extends beyond the boundaries of any single country. This impact may be regional or global in scale.

Possible approaches to answering the question:

Low level of economic development:

One cause of the low level of economic development in Africa is the impact of illness. For example, over half a million people die in sub-Saharan Africa each year because of malaria. Malaria affects families as it reduces their ability to save and being ill from malaria means that people are less able to work and provide for themselves and their families. **(2 marks, explanation of a social factor with examples of link between health and underdevelopment)**

Migration:

Europe is experiencing one of the most significant influxes of migrants and refugees in its history. Pushed by civil war and terror and pulled by the promise of a better life, hundreds of thousands of people have fled the Middle East and Africa, risking their lives along the way. The scale of the crisis has put huge pressures on some destination countries, particularly Greece, Austria and Hungary. At least 350,000 migrants crossed the EU's borders in January–August 2015, compared with just 280,000 during the whole of 2014. **(2 marks, KU)**

The violence in Syria began in March 2011 and the country has been crippled by a brutal civil war ever since. Since then, the United Nations estimates more than 200,000 people have died in the clashes between President Bashar al-Assad's government and rebel forces who want him out. The UN's Refugee Agency says more than four million people have fled Syria to neighbouring countries. In August 2013, a chemical attack just outside the Syrian capital, Damascus, caused a strong reaction from many countries including America, Britain and France. The conflict has been further complicated by the rise of the group Islamic State in 2014. Lots of countries are continuing to supply aid, such as food and emergency supplies, but the US and Britain said they had to stop all other support as they feared the equipment may be stolen by rebel groups, who they did not support. This conflict, together with violence and destruction and the inability to meet their basic needs, has led to the refugee crisis happening in Europe at the moment. **(6 marks, 4 KU with 2 marks analysis)**

5d	12	Analyse the role of national governments in trying to resolve the world issue you have studied. Candidates can be credited in a number of ways up to a maximum of 12 marks. **Credit reference to aspects of the following:** **World issues** • International terrorism • War/conflict • Development/poverty in Africa • Immigration **Terrorism in the UK** • Contest strategy • Role of the police • MI5 **Reference to USA** • War on terror • Use of drones • Hunt for Osama bin Laden Any other valid point that meets the criteria described in the general marking principles for this type of question.
		An analysis mark should be awarded where a candidate uses their knowledge and understanding/a source to identify relevant components (e.g. of an idea, theory, argument, etc.) and clearly shows at least one of the following: • Links between different components. • Links between component(s) and the whole. • Links between component(s) and related concepts. • Similarities and contradictions. • Consistency and inconsistency. • Different views/interpretations. • Possible consequences/implications. • The relative importance of components. • Understanding of underlying order or structure. **Credit responses that make reference to:** • Attempts by national government to resolve the world issue in relation to their country and others. • An analysis of the implications and success of tackling the issue.

Possible approaches to answering the question:

War on terror:

After the 9/11 attacks the USA, along with its allies, led the War on Terror. It entered Afghanistan in order to rid the country of the Al-Qaeda supporting Taliban government. **(1 mark, KU)** *Critics of the USA say this has made the situation worse and made the area more unstable. A new threat has appeared in the form of the ISIL group who have captured and beheaded many Western civilians. However, it could be argued that Afghanistan is more democratic and has more human rights than before.* **(2 marks, analysis)**

(3 marks total)

Migration/Refugees:

The conflict in Syria has seen a massive amount of refugees enter Europe. EU countries such as Germany, Austria and Greece have been overwhelmed by the sheer numbers of people arriving in their country and how to support them – 1.5 million refugees are thought to have arrived by illegal methods alone. There has been a call for greater sharing of this burden over all EU countries, however this has not been without problems. Sweden has had to close its borders to refugees as it feels it can't cope. The UK has agreed to accept 20,000 refugees over the 5 years from 2015. However, this has been met with criticism as some other countries feel this isn't enough. Many UK residents feel the government shouldn't allow these refugees in, as many UK residents are in more need of the help, and they worry that we are opening the door to terrorists. **(5 marks, 3 knowledge, 2 analysis)**

Up to 8 marks for KU (description, explanation and exemplification) and up to 4 marks for analytical comments.

Award up to 6 marks per point.

Where a candidate makes more analytical points than are required to gain the maximum allocation of 4 marks, these can be credited as knowledge and understanding marks provided they meet the criteria for this.

Candidates may make reference to any world issue the impact of which extends beyond the boundaries of any single country. This impact may be regional or global in scale.

Mark Scheme for Exam C

Section 1: Democracy in Scotland and the UK

Question	General marking instructions for this type of question	Max. mark	Specific marking instructions for this question
1	The candidate is required to interpret/evaluate up to three complex sources in order to reach conclusions. In order to achieve credit candidates must show evidence that explains the conclusions reached. • Award up to 3 marks for appropriate use of evidence depending on the quality of the explanation and the synthesis of the evidence to reach any one conclusion. • For full marks candidates must refer to all sources in their answer. • For full marks candidates must reach conclusions about each of the points given and make an overall conclusion on the issue.	8	What conclusions can be drawn about the 2015 General Election campaign after the party leaders' TV debate? Candidates can be credited in a number of ways up to a maximum of 8 marks. **Possible approaches to answering the question:** **The party leader that performed the best in the TV debates:** *The party leader that performed the best in the TV debates could be Nicola Sturgeon. From Source A: 'Nicola Sturgeon was hailed … for her assured performance and suddenly found herself on the national stage' and 'political enemies admitted that she was the biggest winner in the TV debate.'* **(1 mark)** *He party leader that performed the best in the TV debates could be Nicola Sturgeon. From Source A, Labour's Diane Abbott admitted 'Good to see Nicola Sturgeon taking Nigel Farage to task on immigration.' This is backed up by source C, which shows an opinion poll from YouGov taken after the debate. Respondents were asked who they thought performed the best in the TV debates and Sturgeon came out a resounding winner with 28% of the vote; Farage, Cameron and Miliband came second with similar amounts of votes but roughly 10% behind. However from Source A it should be noted that in 3 out of the 4 other opinion polls after the debate Ed Miliband came out top.* **(3 marks, synthesis between sources A and C and a conclusion)**

The party or parties thought likely at the time to form the government after the election:

From Source A, based on opinion polls taken straight after the TV debates, Labour is thought to be most likely to win the 2015 election although not with a majority of more than 326. Source B shows that Labour are predicted to win the UK General Election with 293 seats and MPs, with Conservatives trailing behind with 273. This shows that no party will gain an overall majority. **(1 mark)** *A possible coalition partner could be the SNP as they are predicted to get 48 seats together with the Greens and Plaid Cymru. Source A says 'the SNP would back Labour in a minority government but it would not be a formal coalition which happened with the Conservatives and Lib Dems in 2010.'* **(1 mark)** *The SNP go on to say that they 'would not vote with Labour' as long as they got some things in return such as increased public spending. Ed Miliband has ruled out a formal coalition with Labour. Some estimates put the SNP vote in Scotland as high as 50% so they might have the support.* **(1 mark)**

(3 marks total)

Possible overall conclusion:

From looking at Sources A–C it can be concluded that Nicola Sturgeon of the SNP has become much more high profile and popular as a result of the TV debates; much more than you would expect from a leader who only represents one part of the UK. **(1 mark)** *The 2015 election result as shown by opinion polls is looking very close with no one outright winner and may result in a minority government with voting links with another party or another coalition.* **(1 mark)**

(2 marks total)

Please note that a valid conclusion that is not supported with relevant source evidence should be given no credit.

2a	Evaluation involves making a judgement based on criteria, drawing conclusions on the extent to which a view is supported by the evidence; counter-arguments including possible alternative interpretations; the overall impact/significance of the factors when taken together; the relative importance of factors in relation to the context. **Credit responses that make reference to:** • Different ways in which people can influence the government. • Evaluation of the success of their influence on the government. Up to 8 marks for KU (description, explanation and exemplification) and up to 4 marks for evaluative comments. Award up to 6 marks per point. Candidates should be credited up to full marks if they answer within a Scottish context only, a UK context only or refer to both Scotland and the UK. Where a candidate makes more evaluative points than are required to gain the maximum allocation of 4 marks, these can be credited as knowledge and understanding marks provided they meet the criteria for this.	
	Evaluate the view that current electoral systems used to elect representatives should be changed. Candidates can be credited in a number of ways up to a maximum of 12 marks. **Credit reference to aspects of the following:** • FPTP – used to elect MPs to the House of Commons and the UK government through constituencies. ○ Usually gives strong majority government without the need for coalitions but with minority results in constituencies and overall but may leave voters unrepresented with their votes 'wasted'. ○ Gives disproportionate result – unfair to smaller parties where vote is more spread out and favours Labour, Conservatives and SNP in Scotland. ○ Constituency representation and accountability. ○ Established system that voters are familiar with – referendum in 2011 saw two-thirds of voters wanting to keep FPTP over a PR system. • AMS – used to elect MSPs to Scottish Parliament and Scottish Government. ○ 73 out of 129 MSPs elected to constituencies through FPTP, the remaining 56 elected through a party list system which makes up for the disproportionality by awarding parties with additional members. ○ Voters elect these two kinds of MSPs through two different ballot papers offering choice – smaller parties and independent candidates benefit from this, e.g. the Green Party. ○ Coalitions encouraged, however SNP have a majority government.	12

- ○ Less straightforward system for voters to understand although they are well represented with 8 MSPs.
- ○ Confusion by electorate and 'turf wars' may occur over list versus constituency MSPs.

Any other valid point that meets the criteria described in the general marking principles for this type of question.

Possible approaches to answering the question:

FPTP is used to elect MPs to the House of Commons and thus, the UK government. The party that wins the most MPs wins the General Election and forms the government. Usually a majority government is formed where the winning party is able to ensure that they can pass policies into law as stated in their manifesto. In May 2015, the Conservatives won with a majority unlike in 2010 where they had to form a coalition with the Liberal Democrats and compromise their policies. **(2 marks, KU with exemplification)**

AMS is used to elect MSPs to the Scottish Parliament. It was specifically chosen as an electoral system when the Scottish Parliament was set up to encourage 'power sharing' through coalitions. **(1 mark, KU)** *This was supposed to encourage parties to work together to govern Scotland as opposed to the opposition parties in Westminster. This worked well in the first two terms of the Scottish Parliament as Scottish Labour and Liberal Democrats supposedly worked well in coalition.* **(1 mark, KU)** *However with the rise of support for the SNP they have governed Scotland first with a minority government in 2007 and then with a majority government since 2011. This has allowed them to dominate the Scottish Parliament without the need for consultation with other parties.* **(1 mark, KU)** *This domination has called for some people to argue that the electoral system used to elect the Scottish Parliament should be changed as it fails to deliver one of the founding principles of the Scottish Parliament.* **(1 mark, evaluation)**

(4 marks total)

2b	12	Evaluate the view that the Scottish Parliament needs more powers from the UK Parliament to govern Scotland. Candidates can be credited in a number of ways up to a maximum of 12 marks. **Credit reference to aspects of the following:** • Current devolved powers of the Scottish government. • Current powers reserved to the UK Parliament. • Calls for change following the Independence Referendum/General Election. • Recommendations of the Smith Commission. • UK government's likelihood of granting powers. • Tax raising powers granted from 2017. • Possibility of another referendum on independence. Any other valid point that meets the criteria described in the general marking principles for this type of question. **Possible approaches to answering the question:** *The Scottish Parliament is responsible for making laws on devolved matters. One devolved matter is education. It is responsible for all issues to do with education such as deciding on the Curriculum for Excellence syllabus for ages 3–18, funding for new schools and teachers' pay and conditions. One reserved matter is social security – the UK government decides what benefits are payable to all UK citizens, such as the introduction of Universal Credit. (2 marks, KU)* *The UK government implemented the bedroom tax in all parts of the UK against the wishes of the Scottish government as it is felt that it has caused great hardship to the people of Scotland and demonstrates one reason why people feel that Scotland should have more power over their own welfare and benefits. (3 marks total, knowledge, including evaluative statement)*

Evaluation involves making a judgement based on criteria, drawing conclusions on the extent to which a view is supported by the evidence; counter-arguments including possible alternative interpretations; the overall impact/significance of the factors when taken together; the relative importance of factors in relation to the context.

Credit responses that make reference to:

- The current powers of the Scottish Parliament as devolved from UK government.
- Evaluation of how much power this represents.
- Up to 8 marks for KU (description, explanation and exemplification) and up to 4 marks for evaluative comments. Award up to 6 marks per point.

Candidates should be credited up to full marks if they answer within a Scottish context only, a UK context only or refer to both Scotland and the UK. Where a candidate makes more evaluative points than are required to gain the maximum allocation of 4 marks, these can be credited as knowledge and understanding marks provided they meet the criteria for this.

Since the close Independence Referendum result in September 2014 and the resounding General Election success for the SNP in May 2015, there have been calls for the Scottish parliament to be given more powers. The Smith Commission was set up after the referendum and as a result of the overpowering support for the SNP in the General Election, will be implemented in full. In addition to the current devolved powers, the Scottish parliament will have complete power to set income tax rates and bands. Holyrood will receive a proportion of the VAT raised in Scotland, amounting to the first 10 percentage points of the standard rate. It will have control over a number of benefits including disability living allowance, the personal independence payment, winter fuel payments and the housing elements of Universal Credit, including the 'bedroom tax'. As a result, the powers of the Scottish parliament in relation to the UK parliament have dramatically increased. From SNP supporters there is a call for yet more powers to be given to Scotland. **(4 marks, 3 KU, 1 evaluation)**

Section 2: Social Issues in the UK

Question	General marking instructions for this type of question	Max. mark	Specific marking instructions for this question

3a	An analysis mark should be awarded where a candidate uses their knowledge and understanding/a source to identify relevant components (e.g. of an idea, theory, argument, etc.) and clearly shows at least one of the following:
	
	• Links between different components.
	• Links between component(s) and the whole.
	• Links between component(s) and related concepts.
	• Similarities and contradictions.
	• Consistency and inconsistency.
	• Different views/interpretations.
	• Possible consequences/implications.
	• The relative importance of components.
	• Understanding of underlying causes or structure.
	
	Evaluation involves making a judgement based on criteria, drawing conclusions on the extent to which a view is supported by the evidence; counter-arguments including possible alternative
		20	To what extent is it the responsibility of the government to deal with inequalities?
			
			Candidates can be credited in a number of ways up to a maximum of 20 marks.
			
			Credit reference to aspects of the following:
			
			• **Individualist theories**
			
			  ○ Focus on the responsibility of the individual in making good lifestyle choices in relation to health, income and wealth.
			
			  ○ Making work pay as opposed to relying on benefits.
			
			  ○ Refer to the current (2016) Conservative government and its approach to welfare reform.
			
			  ○ Health – individuals are responsible for their own overuse of drugs and alcohol, unhealthy diet, excessive smoking, lack of engagement in exercise and health prevention services.
			
			• **Collectivist theories**
			
			  ○ Focus is on the role of the state through the welfare state and how much of a role it should play. Reference to the original welfare state and the argument the government needs to correct wealth inequalities by looking at employment and low pay as well as the benefit system.
			
			  ○ Current (2016) Scottish Government approach – e.g. free tuition (no fees).
			
			  ○ Current (2016) UK Labour party and its anti-austerity message.

    ○ Differing responses to health inequalities.

Any other valid point that meets the criteria described in the general marking principles for this type of question.

Possible approaches to answering the question:

The current UK Conservative government at Westminster's approach is to cut the welfare bill and try and get as many people in work as possible. Two examples showing where welfare has been cut are through the benefit cap at £23,000 per year and proposed cuts to tax credits. Working has been made more attractive by raising the tax threshold and the requirement of employers to pay the Living Wage. However, some people feel this approach is too drastic and has worsened poverty as demonstrated by the existence of food banks as a sign of government failure: they have not done enough to help the poor in society. **(3 marks, 2 KU, 1 analysis)**

Poverty plays a large role in health. People living in poor quality housing on limited funds through low pay or unemployment benefits may suffer ill-health due to damp and poorly ventilated conditions. Their diet may consist more of frozen and tinned goods due to long shelf life and ease of cooking. **(2 marks, knowledge)** *Living in stressful, insecure conditions may also affect health as Harry Burns' 'Biology of Poverty' argues – living in chaotic conditions may affect children's nervous system and their ability to fight off diseases in later life. Those living in poverty are more likely to make poor lifestyle decisions such as smoking and drinking to excess. For example, 55% of adults smoke in Easterhouse in Glasgow which is a deprived area, compared to 15% of adults in Glasgow Kelvinside and illnesses from smoking reflect this. From an individualist point of view, it is up to them to change their own behaviour with encouragements such as smoking bans and high taxation on smoking and alcohol. From a collectivist point of view, it is up to the government in the long term to tackle poverty through improving skills, employment opportunities and housing.* **(4 marks, analysis with exemplification)**

(6 marks total)

---

interpretations; the overall impact/ significance of the factors when taken together; the relative importance of factors in relation to the context.

Credit reference to:

- Relevant theories to explain why health inequalities exist.

- Analysis of these theories.

- Balanced overall evaluative comment on the extent to which these theories explain health inequalities.

- Provide a clear, coherent line of argument.

Up to 8 marks for KU (description, explanation and exemplification) and up to 12 marks for analytical/evaluative comments. Award up to 6 marks per point.

Where a candidate makes more analytical/evaluative points than are required to gain the maximum allocation of 4 marks, these can be credited as knowledge and understanding marks provided they meet the criteria for this.

Candidates should be credited up to full marks if they answer within a Scottish context only, a UK context only or refer to both Scotland and the UK.

3b	20	Discuss the impact of income inequality on a group in society you have studied.

Candidates can be credited in a number of ways up to a maximum of 20 marks.

Credit reference to aspects of the following:

- Gender – social exclusion, effects of lone parenthood, effects on health, effect on children through education.

- Race – social exclusion, effect on education.

- The elderly – social exclusion, effects on health.

Any other valid point that meets the criteria described in the general marking principles for this type of question.

Possible approaches to answering the question:

Whilst some pensioners are able to live full lives due to having a good pension funded from a well-paid job and have been able to save, this is not the case for all. 16% of pensioners suffer through having been unemployed through their lives or not having worked for other reasons, and so may have to live off the state pension and benefits alone. One effect of this can be on their health. Those living on a low income, especially in Scotland, may suffer in the cold weather due to not being able to afford to heat their homes because of the cost of heating bills or the perceived cost. Many will miss out on food due to this – this is one of the reasons why the government introduced the Cold Weather Payment.

(3 marks, 1 knowledge, 2 analysis) |

An analysis mark should be awarded where a candidate uses their knowledge and understanding/a source to identify relevant components (e.g. of an idea, theory, argument, etc.) and clearly shows at least one of the following:

- Links between different components to which a view is supported by the evidence.

- The relative importance of factors.

- Counter-arguments including possible alternative interpretations.

- The overall impact/significance of the factors when taken together.

- The relative importance of factors in relation to the context.

Evaluation involves making a judgement based on criteria, drawing conclusions on the extent to which a view is supported by the evidence; counter-arguments including possible alternative interpretations; the overall impact/ significance of the factors when taken together; the relative importance of factors in relation to the context.

Credit reference to:

- The impact of income inequalities.

- An analysis of the effects of income inequalities. | |

	Women are one group who are vulnerable to poverty. Women may struggle on low pay or on benefits as they are the ones who are most likely to be lone parents and have to bear the burden of bringing up a child on their own. Roughly a quarter of families with children are lone parents. They are most likely to be surviving on benefits or working in a low paid job such as one in the 5Cs that fit around school hours. This can be a real struggle and many parents report going without in order to feed their children. **(2 marks, knowledge with some analysis)** *This may have health effects as more women report depression through having to cope with stressful lives and may result in poorer lifestyle choices such as smoking to excess. Having to survive on a low income can have negative effects on their children as they may feel excluded from what other children have. They may miss out on the latest fashionable trainers or on school excursions. Although the risk has fallen in recent years, lone-parent families are twice as likely to be living in relative poverty compared to two-parent families.* **(3 marks, knowledge and some analysis)** **(5 marks total)**	• Balanced overall evaluative comment on the impact of income inequalities for the group you have studied. • Provide a clear, coherent line of argument. Up to 8 marks for KU (description, explanation and exemplification) and up to 12 marks for analytical/evaluative comments. Award up to 6 marks per point. Where a candidate makes more analytical/evaluative points than are required to gain the maximum allocation of 4 marks, these can be credited as knowledge and understanding marks provided they meet the criteria for this.
3c	20	To what extent are social explanations of crime more valid than individualist theories of crime? Candidates can be credited in a number of ways up to a maximum of 20 marks. **Credit reference to aspects of the following:** • Individualist theories to explain crime – white collar crime and greed. • Collectivist theories to explain crime – poverty. Any other valid point that meets the criteria described in the general marking principles for this type of question.	An analysis mark should be awarded where a candidate uses their knowledge and understanding/a source to identify relevant components (e.g. of an idea, theory, argument, etc.) and clearly shows at least one of the following: • Links between different components. • Links between component(s) and the whole.

Possible approaches to answering the question:

Collectivist theories put the cause of crime on the economic conditions in society. Those that cannot achieve material success will commit crime in order to achieve status and material goods. The majority of those who were involved in the London Riots in 2011 and took part in the looting were less well educated and on benefits which lends credit to this theory. **(2 marks, relevant knowledge and analysis)**

Individualist theories focus on the individual's freedom of choice in whether or not they commit crime. One such theory is that of right realism. These theorists reject the idea that poverty is to blame, giving examples such as the fact that in the 1930s there was very little crime but huge unemployment and the fact that since the 1960s crime started to rise with very little unemployment. Given the lack of a link with unemployment, the new right turned to a cultural explanation. They see a decline in 'family values', in particular a lack of discipline both inside and outside the home. In addition, blame is put on the welfare state, which has created a dependency culture and a poor work ethic. In addition, crime is thought to be related to opportunity and choice – people will commit crime if they have the opportunity to do so and they will benefit from it. As a result governments from the 1980s onwards have focused on reducing opportunities for people to commit crime by introducing surveillance measures such as CCTV and making punishments tougher by imprisoning more people. **(6 marks, 3 knowledge, 3 analysis)**

- Links between component(s) and related concepts.
- Similarities and contradictions.
- Consistency and inconsistency.
- Different views/interpretations.
- Possible consequences/implications.
- The relative importance of components.
- Understanding of underlying order or structure.

Evaluation involves making a judgement based on criteria, drawing conclusions on the extent to which a view is supported by the evidence; counter-arguments including possible alternative interpretations; the overall impact/significance of the factors when taken together; the relative importance of factors in relation to the context.

Credit responses that make reference to:

- Explanation of the possible causes of crime.

- Analysis of the possible causes.

- Balanced overall evaluative comment.

- Provide a clear, coherent line of argument.

Up to 8 marks for KU (description, explanation and exemplification) and up to 12 marks for analytical/ evaluative comments. Award up to 6 marks per point.

Where a candidate makes more analytical/evaluative points than are required to gain the maximum allocation of 4 marks, these can be credited as knowledge and understanding marks provided they meet the criteria for this.

Candidates should be credited up to full marks if they answer within a Scottish context only, a UK context only or refer to both Scotland and the UK.

3d		20

Discuss the social, economic and political impact of crime.

Candidates can be credited in a number of ways up to a maximum of 20 marks.

Credit reference to aspects of the following:

- Social and economic – higher cost of insurance premiums if insurance fraud, which is sometimes seen as victimless crime but costs the economy billions of pounds a year; security measures to prevent crime happening again; pain and suffering coupled with the cost of legal fees, funeral fees; loss of productivity when victims miss work; communities may suffer as a result of crime through lower housing costs and reduced tourism; drug abuse may affect productivity as well as the cost of rehab programmes; the whole cost of running the legal system in Scotland and the UK – staffing in courts, prisons and community sentences.

- Political impact – pressure on government to change laws in response to crime – often fuelled by media, criticism of government, policy on current gun laws.

Any other valid point that meets the criteria described in the general marking principles for this type of question.

Possible approaches to answering the question:

Crime costs the UK £124 billion a year, which is equivalent to £4700 per household in the UK. This figure includes the cost of police investigations, the court system as well as prisons and lost productivity experienced by victims and offenders. Most of this is from violent crime but theft is thought to cost the economy £3 billion. **(2 marks, relevant knowledge and exemplification)**

An analysis mark should be awarded where a candidate uses their knowledge and understanding/a source to identify relevant components (e.g. of an idea, theory, argument, etc.) and clearly shows at least one of the following:

- Links between different components to which a view is supported by the evidence.

- The relative importance of factors.

- Counter-arguments including possible alternative interpretations.

- The overall impact/significance of the factors when taken together.

- The relative importance of factors in relation to the context.

Credit reference to:

- The different social, economic and political impact of crime on the wider community.

- Analysis/significance of these factors.

Up to 8 marks for KU (description, explanation and exemplification) and up to 12 marks for analytical/evaluative comments. Award up to 6 marks per point.

Crime can have a wide impact. It can have a major effect on government policy and the laws that are put into the legislative programme of the government especially if fuelled by media campaigns. Crime can also highlight issues with legislation, which perhaps could be seen to be making crime worse. One example of this is the shooting of 11-year-old Rhys Lawrence in Liverpool whilst playing football outside a pub. A member of the 'Croxteth crew' gang was convicted in December 2008 of the murder and sentenced to life imprisonment. The then Prime Minister, Gordon Brown, came under constant pressure to resolve the issues driving these murders. Commentators highlighted a range of social problems that might be responsible including inner city poverty, family breakdown, and the absence of positive black role models in the UK. The government also faced questions over the apparent availability of guns, which had remained strong despite the handgun ban put in place in 1997. Some commentators also suggested the government's legislation, specifically punishments for carrying a gun, was exacerbating gun crime amongst the young. This led to a lengthy consultation by the Home Secretary Theresa May after which the maximum penalty for illegal importation of firearms was increased to life imprisonment. **(6 marks, detailed knowledge and exemplification and analysis)**

Where a candidate makes more analytical/evaluative points than are required to gain the maximum allocation of 4 marks, these can be credited as knowledge and understanding marks provided they meet the criteria for this.

Section 3: International Issues

Question	General marking instructions for this type of question	Max. mark	Specific marking instructions for this question
4	The candidate is required to interpret/evaluate up to three complex sources of information, detecting and explaining the extent of objectivity. In order to achieve credit candidates must show evidence that supports the extent of accuracy in a given viewpoint.	8	'Social and economic inequalities continue to exist equally in all areas across the EU'. Candidates can be credited in a number of ways up to a maximum of 8 marks. **Evidence that supports the view:**
	• Award up to 3 marks for appropriate use of evidence depending on the quality of the explanation and the synthesis of the evidence for any one explanation of the extent of objectivity.		• Source A – inequality continues to exist over all the EU. • Source A – health inequalities are still a cause for concern for both men and women. • Source A – EU literacy rates are very similar for both men and women. • Source B – lung cancer picture similar across all EU countries shown. • Source C – male/female university entrants similar across all countries shown.
	• For full marks candidates must refer to all sources in their answer.		**Possible responses:**
	• For full marks candidates must make an overall judgement as to the extent of the accuracy of the given statement.		*Source A states that health inequalities continue to cause concern over the whole of the EU. In Source B, it shows that the rates of lung cancer are higher for men than women. This pattern is similar for all the EU countries shown.* **(2 marks)**
	• Maximum of 6 marks if no overall judgement made on extent of accuracy of the statement.		*Source A shows that literacy rates are very similar for males and females in all EU states, as are the numbers of males and females going to university. This is backed up by Source C which shows that the ratios of male/female university entrants are similar in the countries shown, with females making up between 50% and 60% of students in all the countries listed.* **(2 marks)**

Evidence that does not support the view:

- Source A – some of the newer EU countries have made less progress in tackling inequality.
- Source A – differences between countries in terms of the life expectancy gap.
- Source A – richer countries have more women in top boardroom positions.
- Source B – statistics on varying life expectancy in selected EU countries.
- Source B – statistics vary across different countries on heart attacks and strokes.
- Source C – statistics showing differences in top positions.

Possible responses:

Source A states that some EU countries are amongst the most equal in the world, with Germany in 11th place out of 134 in the Global Gender Gap report; however some of the newer countries do less well with the Czech Republic in 75th place and Estonia at 52nd place. **(1 mark)**

Source A states that although average life expectancy and quality of life have increased over the last sixty years, there are still differences between countries. **(1 mark)** *This is backed up by Source B which shows that more developed countries like France and Germany have higher life expectancy than developing countries like the Czech Republic and Estonia. The life expectancy for men in France, for example, is 77 whilst in Estonia it is ten years sooner at 67.* **(3 marks)**

- Candidates may be awarded up to a maximum of 2 marks for incorporating an evaluation of the reliability of the sources in their explanations, although this is not mandatory.

Source A states that in richer countries more women reach top positions, but in all countries they still lag behind men in terms of boardroom representation. This is demonstrated by Source C which shows that this varies between countries – In Germany 17% of top positions are held by women but in Estonia only 7% are. **(2 marks)**

Although average life expectancy and quality of life have increased over the last sixty years, there are still differences between countries. Source A states that certain diseases affect men more than women and this is confirmed by Source B which shows the differences between countries in illness rates. There are much higher rates of stroke and heart disease in the Czech Republic and Estonia compared to France and Germany. **(2 marks)**

Candidates may also be credited up to 2 marks on any comment/ evaluation of the origin and reliability of the sources:

Overall, the sources are not reliable. Although The Independent newspaper is a well-respected broadsheet with a reputation for reliability, it has been adapted so we have no idea if the facts have been distorted. It is also out of date for our purposes – information and progress on equality may have changed. No information is given on the origin of the statistics as although they back up the article, no information is given that could be checked up on. **(2 marks)**

For full marks, candidates must make an overall judgement as to the extent of the accuracy of the given statement:

Overall, the evidence does not support the view as social and economic inequalities continue to exist but are not experienced equally in all areas of the EU. All countries have made progress but from Source A women are still concentrated in low-paid, part-time work and are under-represented in the boardroom. The richer EU countries like France and Germany have made more progress in closing the pay gap and lessening the effects of the glass ceiling. **(2 marks)**

	12	For a world power you have studied, analyse its influence on world affairs by its involvement in international organisations.

Candidates can be credited in a number of ways up to a maximum of 12 marks.

Credit reference to aspects of the following:

- Membership of UN and Security Council
- Membership of NATO
- Membership of G7/G20
- Membership of EU/relationship with it
- Other relevant international organisations such as WTA, OECD, World Bank

Any other valid point that meets the criteria described in the general marking principles for this type of question.

Possible approaches to answering the question:

World power – The USA:

The USA is one of the most important members of the United Nations. Most countries of the world are members of the UN but real power in terms of making decisions about world peace lies in the hands of the Security Council. This is made up of 15 member countries. Five of these are permanent – UK, USA, France, China and Russia and 10 others are temporary – they sit at the table for 2 years before other countries take their turn. As a permanent member, the USA therefore has a lot of influence over what actions the UN takes in the face of a conflict such as that taking place in Syria over the last couple of years. **(3 marks, knowledge with analysis)**

5a

An analysis mark should be awarded where a candidate uses their knowledge and understanding / a source to identify relevant components (e.g. of an idea, theory, argument, etc.) and clearly shows at least one of the following:

- Links between different components.
- Links between component(s) and the whole.
- Links between component(s) and related concepts.
- Similarities and contradictions.
- Consistency and inconsistency.
- Different views/interpretations.
- Possible consequences/implications.
- The relative importance of components.
- Understanding of underlying order or structure.

Credit responses that make reference to:

- Involvement in international organisations.

- Analysis of the extent of influence.

Up to 8 marks for KU (description, explanation and exemplification) and up to 4 marks for analytical comments. Award up to 6 marks per point.

Where a candidate makes more analytical points than are required to gain the maximum allocation of 4 marks, these can be credited as knowledge and understanding marks provided they meet the criteria for this.

Candidates may make reference to any member of the G20 group of countries, excluding the United Kingdom.

World issue – China:

China is one of the most important members of the United Nations. Most countries of the world are members of the UN but real power in terms of making decisions about world peace lies in the hands of the Security Council. This is made up of 15 member countries. Five of these are permanent – UK, USA, France, China and Russia and 10 others are temporary – they sit at the table for 2 years before other countries take their turn. **(2 marks, knowledge)** *As a permanent member, China therefore has a lot of influence over what actions the UN takes in the face of a conflict such as that taking place in Syria over the last couple of years.* **(1 mark, analysis)** *Permanent Security Council members have the right to veto any direct action taken by the UN. China and Russia have, in the past, vetoed direct action against President Al-Assad as they are allies. As a result, the UN have been accused of failing the innocent civilians who have had their lives turned upside down by the raging civil war.* **(1 mark, analysis)** *It is thought that 4 million people have left their homes in Syria and 4 out of 5 people are living in poverty due to the effect on the country.* **(1 mark, knowledge)** *In conclusion, China has a big role in the UN Security Council and its decisions can have a big impact on the lives of people suffering through a conflict situation.* **(1 mark, evaluative comment)**

(6 marks total)

12	An analysis mark should be awarded where a candidate uses their knowledge and understanding/a source to identify relevant components (e.g. of an idea, theory, argument, etc.) and clearly shows at least one of the following:	For a world power you have studied, analyse the nature and extent of socio-economic inequality.

An analysis mark should be awarded where a candidate uses their knowledge and understanding/a source to identify relevant components (e.g. of an idea, theory, argument, etc.) and clearly shows at least one of the following:

- Links between different components.
- Links between component(s) and the whole.
- Links between component(s) and related concepts.
- Similarities and contradictions.
- Consistency and inconsistency.
- Different views/interpretations.
- Possible consequences/implications.
- The relative importance of components.
- Understanding of underlying order or structure.

Credit responses that make reference to:

- The socio-economic inequalities that exist.
- An analysis of these inequalities.

5b / 12

For a world power you have studied, analyse the nature and extent of socio-economic inequality.

Candidates can be credited in a number of ways up to a maximum of 12 marks.

Credit reference to aspects of the following:

- Evidence and explanation of inequality between different groups in society.
- Income, health, education, employment and housing opportunities.
- Explanation of how these things occur.
- Government attempts to tackle inequality and whether successful.

Any other valid point that meets the criteria described in the general marking principles for this type of question.

Possible approaches to answering the question:

The USA:

Blacks and Hispanics are three times more likely to live in poverty in the USA. This is more likely to happen in inner-city areas where there is a lack of encouragement and opportunity to do well in education. Black youths are more likely to go to prison rather than college. They are more likely to attend schools lacking educational facilities and teachers have fewer expectations of them.

(2 marks, relevant knowledge)

China:

The emergence of a middle class, combined with high levels of personal savings and low levels of personal debt, shows evidence of China's new-found wealth. The average wealth per Chinese citizen is $17,126. Looking only at the data for the whole country, however, conceals the growing difference between urban and rural areas. China remains a very rural economy and despite the continued growth in urbanisation, 50.3% of China's population still live in rural areas. In 2010, rural residents had an annual income of 5,900 yuan ($898) compared to urban income at 19,100 yuan ($2,900). Many rural residents have limited access to financial services such as a bank and appliances such as washing machines, which shows the different lifestyles of rural/urban. **(3 marks, 2 KU and 1 analysis)**

At the end of 2009, China had an estimated 229.8 million rural migrant workers, of which about 149 million are thought to work outside their registered home area. The official average monthly wage for these workers, many of whom work in manufacturing and assembly, was 1,417 yuan. Moreover, because these migrants work outside their registered area, the low wage rates conceal enormous personal sacrifices, which include long working hours, poor housing conditions and a loss in welfare benefits associated with the household registration system known as Hukou. The government has recognised these problems and has worked to increase the minimum wage as well as encouraging industries to move to rural areas, however rural inequality continues to have significant impact. **(4 marks, 3 KU, 1 evaluative comment)**

Up to 8 marks for KU (description, explanation and exemplification) and up to 4 marks for analytical comments. Award up to 6 marks per point.

Where a candidate makes more analytical points than are required to gain the maximum allocation of 4 marks, these can be credited as knowledge and understanding marks provided they meet the criteria for this.

Candidates may make reference to any member of the G20 group of countries, excluding the United Kingdom.

5c	An analysis mark should be awarded where a candidate uses their knowledge and understanding/a source to identify relevant components (e.g. of an idea, theory, argument, etc.) and clearly shows at least one of the following: • Links between different components. • Links between component(s) and the whole. • Links between component(s) and related concepts. • Similarities and contradictions. • Consistency and inconsistency. • Different views/interpretations. • Possible consequences/implications. • The relative importance of components. • Understanding of underlying order or structure. **Credit responses that make reference to:** • The factors that have caused the world issue. • An analysis of the consequences of these factors.	
12	For a world issue you have studied, analyse the nature and extent of the issue. Candidates can be credited in a number of ways up to a maximum of 12 marks. **Credit reference to aspects of the following:** • Development in Africa – effects of war, corruption, debt, trade. • Terrorism – nationalism, extreme fundamentalism, right wing views, poverty and lack of democracy as triggers. Any other valid point that meets the criteria described in the general marking principles for this type of question. **Possible approaches to answering the question:** *African countries have suffered from a lack of development as a result of conflict. Many countries in Africa have endured years of civil war, which has meant that public funds have been diverted away from spending on education, infrastructure and healthcare and spent on weapons. For example, Angola has natural resources in the form of diamonds and oil but remains very poor as a result of a 27-year conflict.* **(2 marks, knowledge and analysis)** *Despite having natural resources in the form of diamonds and oil Angola remains very poor as a result of a 27-year-conflict. Since the ceasefire in 2002 Angola has gradually rebuilt its infrastructure, retrieving weapons from its heavily-armed civilian population and resettling tens of thousands of refugees who fled the fighting. However, landmines and impassable roads have hampered the recovery and have cut off large parts of the country. The full impact of landmines on human wellbeing and livelihoods is widespread. These costs cannot be measured in only economic terms; landmines are designed to maim the victim's limbs and reproductive organs and can have severe*	

psychological impacts on those affected. For example, due to prejudice and cultural factors in some communities, injured unmarried women may have reduced opportunities to marry and have children. Landmines are cheap to use but extremely expensive to decommission, which has slowed down the rebuilding process. **(6 marks, 3 knowledge, 3 analysis)**

12	For the world issue you have studied, analyse the effects this issue has had on individuals. Candidates can be credited in a number of ways up to a maximum of 12 marks. **Credit reference to aspects of the following:** • International terrorism – deaths, destruction, increased fearfulness in society, increased security at large scale events, increased security at airports. • Lack of development in African countries – poverty, lack of education and access to properly organised healthcare, death and illness, ruled by corrupt government, lack of access to clean water. Any other valid point that meets the criteria described in the general marking principles for this type of question.

Up to 8 marks for KU (description, explanation and exemplification) and up to 4 marks for analytical comments. Award up to 6 marks per point.

Where a candidate makes more analytical points than are required to gain the maximum allocation of 4 marks, these can be credited as knowledge and understanding marks provided they meet the criteria for this.

Candidates may make reference to any world issue the impact of which extends beyond the boundaries of any single country. This impact may be regional or global in scale.

5d	An analysis mark should be awarded where a candidate uses their knowledge and understanding/a source to identify relevant components (e.g. of an idea, theory, argument, etc.) and clearly shows at least one of the following: • Links between different components. • Links between component(s) and the whole. • Links between component(s) and related concepts. • Similarities and contradictions.

Possible approaches to answering the question:

Terrorism:

In the short term, ordinary people have been affected by horrendous terrorist attacks such as 9/11 in New York, 7/7 in London and the Anders Breivik shootings in Norway. These attacks killed a substantial number of people in each country and created mass hysteria and fear amongst local people. **(2 marks, knowledge and exemplification)**

One effect on ordinary people has been the response to terrorism by national governments. The USA have been criticised for their use of drones (unmanned craft) in Pakistan and Afghanistan in order to hunt down terror cells. However their use in attacking members of Al-Qaeda has led to the death of innocent civilians, notably an American and an Italian aid worker in Pakistan as well as Pakistani civilians. In the 'War on Terror' where the US and allies invaded Afghanistan, many innocent Afghans were caught up in the crossfire. In terms of troops – 453 British troops were killed and many more were injured or maimed. In total, over 3000 coalition troops have been killed – the majority of them American. To conclude, not only have terrorist attacks killed and injured substantial numbers of people, there has also been collateral damage sustained in the attempts to solve terrorism. **(4 marks, 3 knowledge, 1 evaluative comment)**

- Consistency and inconsistency.
- Different views/interpretations.
- Possible consequences/implications.
- The relative importance of components.
- Understanding of underlying order or structure.

Credit responses that make reference to:

- How individuals are affected by the world issue.
- Analysis of the consequences.

Up to 8 marks for KU (description, explanation and exemplification) and up to 4 marks for analytical comments. Award up to 6 marks per point.

Where a candidate makes more analytical points than are required to gain the maximum allocation of 4 marks, these can be allocated knowledge marks provided they meet the criteria.

Candidates may make reference to any world issue the impact of which extends beyond the boundaries of any single country. This impact may be regional or global in scale.

Notes

Notes

Notes

Notes

Notes

Notes

Notes

Notes

Notes

Notes